Her Tongue on My Theory

Her Tongue on My Theory

Images, Essays and Fantasies

KISS & TELL

Persimmon Blackbridge
Lizard Jones
Susan Stewart

Press Gang Publishers
Vancouver

First Printing March 1994
1 2 3 4   98 97 96 95 94

The Publisher gratefully acknowledges financial assistance from the Canada Council and the Cultural Services Branch, Province of British Columbia.

CANADIAN CATALOGUING IN PUBLICATION DATA

Kiss & Tell (Group of Artists)
Her tongue on my theory

ISBN 0-88974-058-5
1. Photography, Erotic. 2. Lesbianism in art. 3. Lesbianism—Fiction.
I. Title.
TR676.K47 1994   779'.28'092   C94-910179-6

Design by Lizard Jones
Edited by Barbara Kuhne
Cover photograph by Susan Stewart
Author photograph by Daniel Collins
Typeset in Minion and Franklin Gothic by The Typeworks

Printed on acid-free paper
Printed and bound in Canada

Press Gang Publishers
#101–225 East 17th Avenue
Vancouver, B.C. V5V 1A6
Canada

Dedicated to the women and men at Little Sister's Bookstore,
for outrageous patience and furious impatience
in their ongoing battle with Canada Customs.

TABLE OF CONTENTS

Acknowledgements

KISS & TELL would like to thank Irit Shimrat and Janine Fuller for their insightful feedback on this manuscript. Also Agnes Huang for her invaluable commentary on "Against the Law" and "Questioning Censorship." Sandra Robinson generously provided computer expertise for which we are most grateful. Thanks to Rob Kozinuk and Western Front for countless hours of technical support on the computer/video images. Our gratitude also to our lawyer, barbara findlay, for knowing the answers to many strange questions, and being there when we need her. And of course this book could not have happened without the vision, dedication, and butt-kicking of the press "gang"—Barbara Kuhne, Della McCreary, and Val Speidel. The intricacies of two collectives working together were breathtaking at times, but Press Gang's patience was exceeded only by their hard work and skill.

PERSIMMON: I would like to thank Shani Mootoo for laughing, reading me stories, and helping me figure stuff out; Lori Lesk for her horrible day in the library looking things up for me; Agnes Huang, again; Jean and Jack Mitten for being so calm about having a lesbian sex artist daughter; Ardyth for taking me on walks even when I had a deadline; Sheila Gilhooly for reality checks; Della McCreary for listening to every draft of every essay, driving me in her car, and knowing what I mean when I don't make sense; Lorna Boschman for remembering my birthday, listening to me bitch, and doing the dishes when it was my turn.

LIZARD: Nothing would be the same (especially not this book) without the continuing hilarity and commitment of my constructed family: my lover Suzo Hickey and her children Marlon and Jessica. The list of friends who have provided much needed distraction is endless, but I have to mention Joelene Clarke, Moira Keigher, Rachel Rocco, and Ivy Scott.

SUSAN: I would like to thank my partner Ali McIlwaine for the many hours she spent with me reading, editing, and exchanging ideas. Her intelligent thinking and emotional support were crucial to my contributions to this book. I am deeply grateful for Hollie Levine's stimulating, encouraging, and constant friendship. Deborah Pike and Stephanie Pobihushchy provided a steady flow of humour and affection. Heartfelt thanks to my daughter Rhea for her patient generosity when my work, all too frequently, cut into our time together.

IMAGES

All pictures appearing on the top two-thirds of the pages were photographed by Susan Stewart, for our performance piece TRUE INVERSIONS.

All pictures appearing on the bottom of the pages were designed by Persimmon Blackbridge, with the exception of the series on pages 40–41, 58–59, 92–93, and 105, which were designed by Susan Stewart and Persimmon Blackbridge. All of these images were taken from video tapes shot for TRUE INVERSIONS, with Kim Blain, Paul Lang, Shani Mootoo, or Pat Feindel on camera, lighting by Paul Lang, directed by Lorna Boschman.

In all images, the models are Persimmon Blackbridge, Lizard Jones, and/or Susan Stewart, with the following exceptions: Ali McIlwaine appears on pages 26–27, 58–59, and 92–93; Shani Mootoo appears on page 40, and Paul Lang appears on page 105.

INTRODUCTION

If HER TONGUE ON MY THEORY had been produced outside Canada, chances are it would never get into our country. It would be seized and held at the border. As lesbian artists who live and work in Canada, one of the few ways in which we can count on seeing sex images and stories is by making them ourselves. This is not a terrible burden for us—we love making representations of our own sexuality. What we don't love is how state censorship denies our rights and threatens our queer culture. Yet this very censorship stimulates us to think of devious and delightful ways to challenge these prohibitions.

It comes as no surprise that books are a primary target for those who would censor. They are produced in large quantities, they are small discrete packages that can be easily hidden, and they contain large and powerful ideas. They can be easily disseminated, passed hand to hand if need be. They have the potential to *reach* people.

Books can break walls. As artists with roots in various queer communities, we are committed to making art that isn't safely confined in the mainstream gallery system. This is one of the concerns that brought us—Persimmon Blackbridge, Lizard Jones, and Susan Stewart—together in Kiss & Tell. As a collective of three lesbian artists, we make art about sex, and sometimes we make sex for art.

HER TONGUE ON MY THEORY comes out of our previous collaborative projects. Our first piece, DRAWING THE LINE, an interactive exhibit of lesbian sexual photographs, has been shown in fifteen cities on three continents. That meant we all did a lot of travelling around, doing public speaking gigs. The best parts of those trips were the late night intense and personal discussions about sex, censorship and life in general, with people we had just met. At the talks and afterwards we heard all kinds of people's ideas and experiences and crazy dreams. A question that stumped us at a presentation in one city often was answered by someone else in another city, and would eventually get written into our artists' talk.

We started this book because a friend convinced us that we should turn some of those talks into essays and make a book out of them. But of course once we started, it was impossible to keep it simple. It always is in Kiss & Tell. First, there were certain things we never actually wrote down because we could rely on covering them in the discussion periods. Also, there were many ideas and issues that women had raised along the way, which we were still trying to understand and come to grips with. That's where our energy was, that's what we wanted to write about—the things we hadn't figured out yet.

So we wrote and met and wrote. And met. HER TONGUE ON MY THEORY is the culmination of lots of tongue wagging—many informal and formal meetings about sexual representation. Each essay marks a coming together, an agreed upon risk, an agreement to disagree. Sometimes the result was such an amalgamation that it had to be attributed to all three of us. Sometimes one of us used those meetings to hone her own particular voice.

In the first essay, "Porn Wars and Other Hysteries," we begin by looking at the lesbian feminist community, *our* community, and why we came together as a group within it. In "Doing It Together" we talk about some of the issues we face as we work together making art about sex—from the process of feminist collaboration, to situating our work on a continuum of transgressive imagery, to working in a world where lesbians are both invisible and hated. "Redemption and Transgression" is about making ourselves palatable. What do we give up? What do we gain from being outsiders? What do we lose?

Many people just wish lesbians would shut up. Kiss & Tell has encountered the right wing in myriad guises, and in "The Abhorrent Lesbian Show" we talk about a specific incident in Alberta, Canada, where our art work was used as the excuse to spread homophobic propaganda of all kinds, and to threaten arts funding.

Back in our own community, the debate about pornography rages on. Should the government be controlling sexual imagery? When is it fighting sexism? When is it censoring queer culture? Persimmon analyzes current anti-porn rulings in "Against the Law." The essay "Questioning Censorship" challenges the terms in which the censorship debate is currently framed, and the alliances we are forced into. Our experiences with both state censorship and community protest have led us to a new imperative: exploring the complexity of whose power, and whose voice.

The perfect feminist way to deal with sexist imagery is not something we have figured out.

In the process of writing these essays, Lizard started saying, "We never talk about sex anymore, we only talk about theory." After she'd said it many times, we finally recognized it as an issue we had to confront, not just a passing complaint about life in Kiss & Tell. The issue was lust. Too often sexual analysis and sexual pleasure are seen as incompatible opposites. Kiss & Tell has always delighted in making art that mixes them up. It's one of our favourite things. However, the essay format didn't seem to have much room for indulging in unredeemed pleasure.

But lust was not lost. Persimmon came up with the idea of us all writing sex stories. The hero of these stories is an unidentified Kiss & Tell gal who seems to do a lot of theorizing, and needs the intervention of a Mysterious Woman to put her back in touch with living, breathing sex. Sound familiar? Recycling our lives into artwork.

What is their relationship to each other, the essays and stories? They inform each other, the way sex informs our reactions to imagery, and political theory informs our sexual lives. This book comes from many places at once: refusing the separation of sexual representation and its analysis; mingling lust, intellect, and personal history.

Kiss & Tell is a group with roots firmly in visual art, yet here we were writing endlessly. Could a book be anything like an art piece? Susan suggested adding images to make a "book work," an art piece in book form that would combine the pleasures of reading, thinking, and looking.

The pictures in this book amplify both the fantasies and the analysis. All are taken from a video and performance piece called TRUE INVERSIONS. The large single images are from a series of slides that, in the performance, are projected on stage behind the three of us as we read separate but overlapping porn/sex stories. The series of images at the bottom of the pages are stills and outtakes from the video, combined into new sequences. In both cases the images are of ourselves. They do not illustrate the stories or the essays, but run parallel to them, questioning the same issues of erotic representation, narrative, literal meaning, and censorship.

As we write in the first essay, "It all comes at us at once, not neatly separated out." Like when we're sitting in Persimmon's kitchen, we talk about it all at once. We get ideas, make big plans, and throw caution to the wind.

PORN WARS AND OTHER HYSTERIES

We experience the contradiction. We understand the seduc-
tion. We understand the contradiction. We experience the
seduction.

—SUR MEHAT[1]

Surviving the seventies

SUSAN: I remember clearly the moment when I first held Monique Wittig's book *The Lesbian Body*[2] in my hands. It was the seventies, in Calgary, and it was as if I was seeing that title from some far distant place, through some kind of mental and emotional fog. The Lesbian Body; the sheer boldness of those words was stunning. Who would be brave enough to keep this book on the coffee table? I was, because I didn't have anything to lose. I was straight. A straight radical feminist artist. Books with dangerous-sounding titles had a lot of currency in my crowd. Yet this book was having a marked and decidedly different effect on me, and I hadn't even got past the title.

With some premonition I sensed that this text had an edge on all the other radical texts I had come across. Somehow I knew, even then, that to comprehend the meaning of this text, to approach this unknown world where a lesbian body existed, would require a definite separation from the world I knew. Witness the faint tremor in the hands, the thin veil of sweat starting to cover my

1. Sur Mehat; artist's statement for "sixbooks for public and private usage"; exhibited at Women in Focus Gallery, Vancouver, B.C., 1992.

2. Monique Wittig, *The Lesbian Body* (New York: Avon Books, 1975).

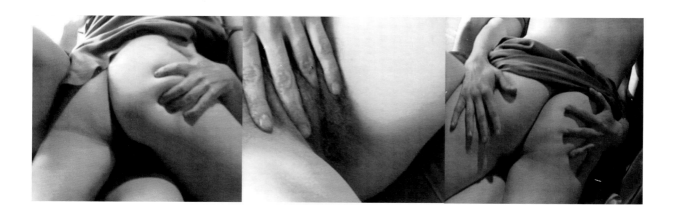

body, my rapidly beating heart. Surely these symptoms were telling me something, something I can say now but couldn't say then. That the very hands that held those texts were lesbian hands, that those legs, arms, breasts, cunt, feet, hips were lesbian, that the mind attached to that body was a lesbian mind, thinking lesbian thoughts, seditious and rebellious lesbian thoughts.

This was a truth impossible to acknowledge. This internal outing, this epiphany of the spirit was happening to a heterosexual woman whose childhood had been one of thorough indoctrination in both Christian morality and institutionalized familial responsibility. An indoctrination so complete that the mere idea of refusing that role, of living without a man brought intense thoughts of fear, retribution, and unmitigated peril. There was no way on earth that I could verbally articulate this insurrection that was brewing at the depths of my being. Mere speech felt far too hazardous. The way I and the women I worked with found to describe this and other contradictions in our lives was by making pictures, photographs.

PERSIMMON: Back in the seventies, anti-porn analysis reigned supreme in the feminist movement, and I was a for sure feminist. Feminism had broken me out of a long, hard breakdown and I was never going to feel that bad again. I was saved. I was a new convert to the adventure of feminism, full of passionate ideas and unexamined arrogance; a born-again lesbian, making right-on art about right-on sex: pure theory.

If what we don't *like is man-made images of subservient women in lacy underwear, then what we* do *like must be perfectly naked lesbians, with equal haircuts. If this one's touching that one's cunt, then that one better be touching this one's cunt, at the same time, in the same way, or else it's not True Equality.*

I made a lot of sculptures of women floating in the air, because perfect mutuality was otherwise anatomically impossible.

But nothing is ever that simple. At the same time as I was making theoretical

NOTE ON LANGUAGE
These days, many people seem to use the word "pornography" to mean sexual images that they don't like and "erotica" to mean sexual images that they do like. This is confusing, since we all have such different opinions. It also makes invisible the class biases intertwined with those words. In this book, we use the words pornography, erotica, and sexual imagery interchangeably.

art, my sex life was more complicated. My lover at the time was a retired sex worker who had come out in the sixties, in a bar scene where drag queens, dykes, and prostitutes hung out together and watched each others' backs. What was *she* doing with *me*? I guess despite my naiveté, we did have some things in common. Neither of us had ever identified as heterosexual. Both of us had been through the psychiatric system, her as an inmate and me as an outpatient. We were both artists, and both alcoholics.

Sex between us was sweet, terrifying, and wild.

The feeling of our sex was *not* what I was calling up when I made those sculptures. Why didn't I notice that the sex I was having and the sex I was portraying were so different? Why didn't I pay attention to how sex *really felt* when I was making those flying fucks? Shame, I guess. Shame so deep I couldn't look it in the face. *Sometimes even the softest of sex scared me. Other times rape fantasies turned me on. Sometimes I pretended my lover was a guy.*

Let's be clear about this: it wasn't feminists who taught me sexual shame. I learned it long before, under harder hands. By the time I was a teenager I had already learned to disconnect from my body. How I felt didn't matter. Sex wasn't about how I felt. It was about doing what I was told. Trying not to gag when my gentle boyfriend came in my mouth; pretending I was turned on when I wasn't or pretending I wasn't when I was; pretending I didn't see the tied-up girl in the porn mag; pretending I didn't know her, want her, want to be her. *Because if you want that (they say), you will be telling men that rape is fun (they say), you will be asking for it (they say). Good Girls look the other way.*

The feminist movement gave me far more than its faults. It gave me hope, pride, work, a place to stand. But sometimes it seemed no different from where I grew up. You had to pretend and not notice you were pretending. You had to shut up and swallow it.

So I went to those meetings and kept my mouth shut when some of the bad pictures in the anti-porn slide shows turned me on. I learned the lines, but they

HALIFAX

" . . . claim its rightful place as a passionate alternative on the spectrum of human relations."

Click. The slide projector is off, the Kiss & Tell talk is over, and the lights come up. Thank God. I did nothing but fuck up tonight, transposing words, reversing slides for a while before giggles in the audience tipped me off. And then that last one ended up being on the screen forever. I'm tired.

But there's still the questions to come.

Smile.

"Are you turned on when you do those photos?"

"Are the comments different in each city?"

"Is it true that condom testing is inadequate?"

I'm really on automatic pilot. I feel like I'm ripping them off, but what more do they want? I don't feel generous, I feel vulnerable. I don't feel strong, I feel a wall go up. Smile. I can talk about

Is this

a nude or is it

my body?

anything to anybody and still smile! I can talk about being turned on like it's a tap! I can discuss safer sex, and *Penthouse* magazine, and hate literature! I have prepared statements about lesbian love, and penetration, and butch/femme, and sado-masochism! I'm well versed in history and science fiction and laws and everything! I am super feminist porn star, and I am tired.

I feel a pair of eyes boring into me from the front row. I look down, but I know before I see her that she's trouble. She's slouching and confident, and smirking just a bit, like she can see through the porn star act. She has her hand up. I smile, and I can feel myself blushing already. I try to wipe my forehead casually like it's hot under the lights and you don't understand the trials of the stars, but I am worried that I just look like I am blushing.

"Do you think the explicitness of an image is linked to how well it expresses desire?" she asks. She dwells on the word desire just a smidge longer than necessary.

Or is that her accent?

didn't fit my life. And I hadn't learned my sexuality from porn. I had learned it from cartoons, commercials, and comic books. I had learned it from the everyday violence of childhood. I wasn't Good, I was a complex mixture of rebellion, analysis, and internalized sexism.

These were things you couldn't talk about, back then, without fear of losing your feminist membership card. The best I ever got was a condescending lecture from some nouveau dyke about not giving in to my male-identified conditioning. It was years before I found a place where I could admit to my sexual contradictions.

LIZARD: In the seventies, while many of my friends were already wrestling with feminism, I was in high school, wrestling with sex. It turned out the feminist community was a lot like high school in some ways. With some high school friends, it was assumed you knew what a blow job was; with other friends you wouldn't think of using the words. But who could you ask? Later, among feminists, there were groups where you couldn't admit you had never been tied up, and groups where reviling bondage constituted small talk. No one agreed, but everyone seemed sure their own position was right. It was a tricky time for the curious.

I came into the women's movement in 1982, at a time when feminists my age (twenty) were rebelling against what was perceived as impossible dogma on the part of older (in their thirties by this time) feminists. I wore miniskirts to work at the feminist newspaper and this was a sign of my rebellion. I scoffed at square lesbians, separatist lesbians, flaky lesbians. I listened to The Slits, The Clash, Marianne Faithfull, and Patti Smith instead of Holly Near and Meg Christian. I read lesbian sex magazines.

At the same time I was trying to get men in anarchist/peace/anti-prison groups to recognize that sexism existed in their groups too. Often this took the form of getting the group to take a stand against pornography. It was the most visible feminist issue of the time. It challenged the media. And we were all

Who is this woman?

My cunt is reacting and the blush has not left my face. I fumble. I drop my papers and the slide remote.

"Sorry," I say as I bend down to pick them up.

"I can wait," she says.

Eventually the answer comes out. She's not listening, anyway, just looking at me. Still waiting. I turn away.

There's a hand up at the very back. "Yeah?" I ask and smile.

"I disagree with what you said about the Butler decision," this one says. "It's a victory for feminists to finally have a law that addresses the degradation and humiliation in sexist imagery. I think you should acknowledge that it is a victory, and not be so critical of it."

She's a few years older than me, and full of that angry self-assurance that pulled me into feminism in the first place. Even as I reply, pointing out how Butler has been used repeatedly against lesbians and gays, I feel like I am missing something too.

against it, weren't we? I see now that part of why it was accepted as an issue was that men could be against porn and still have sexist relationships, worksites, and meetings. All they had to do was not have the magazines. Politics made easy.

I thought lesbian magazines were different, but just like I knew to keep *Playboy* hidden from my parents, I knew to keep *On Our Backs* out of the women's centre, and out of the peace march. It felt like the same fears were at work, even though the situations were supposedly so different. And my lover, and my friends, kept disagreeing with me about everything.

Lots happened in the eighties. For one thing, women with more courage and sexual confidence than me took their *On Our Backs* to feminist places and began talking. Feminist debates about porn became more and more entrenched. I gave up on the men of the fringe left and focussed on lesbian issues and lesbian concerns.

But I was still silenced, now because I was a fence-sitter, and there was no room for fence-sitters in our movement. By the late eighties, the split was there, the sex radicals vs. the feminists, the male-identified vs. the prudes.

In the trenches

KISS & TELL: Part of our community is fighting *for* state censorship of sexual imagery, in the form of anti-porn legislation, and part of our community is struggling *against* homophobic suppression of gay and lesbian sex. Sometimes both parts are in the same person.

Kiss & Tell's roots are in the anti-pornography movement. We were all three anti-porn activists at one time or another. We picketed porn shops by day, and spray-painted them with anti-porn slogans by night. We organized events, did door-to-door education, and made posters for various groups. We knew where we stood (or pretended to). Porn was bad and we were good and people who were worried about censorship were labelled as old-fashioned liberal free speechers or selfish, sexist gay men.

So what happened? How did we lose our answers and end up with endless questions?

All of our lives, we three (and perhaps some of you, also) have lived in this strange culture where we are taught to see the world in a very linear, binary fashion. True and false, yes and no, right and wrong, good girls and bad girls. But life comes at us from a hundred different directions at once. Points of view collide, separate truths contradict each other.

If we look at our sexuality from one point of view, we feel that sex is empowering. We affirm our sexuality, we celebrate it. From another point of view, we recognize that we have been victims of sexism and sexual violence. We want to be protected from sexual images.

Sometimes in debates about pornography and censorship we are acknowledged only as victims, or only as self-affirming sexual subjects. Other times, everything that is painful is defined as male and everything that is joyous is defined as female, and we are urged to reclaim our "natural" female sexuality, as if it existed untouched under the layers of pain, shame, and fear. As if our sexist conditioning were a T-shirt with a slogan we were tired of, that we could just whip off, and feel the sun and wind on our naked breasts.

But if it's a T-shirt, it was put on long ago, over open wounds. Our flesh has healed around it, only to be wounded again and again. It is part of us, grown into our scars. And yet we have joy. It all comes at us at once, not neatly separated out. Sexual abuse, male violence, repression, pleasure, sexism, friendship, love, racism, state control of our bodies and our art, political disagreements, television . . . all these things are part of our sexuality.

In this strange culture, being nice girls has been our safety and our trap. Women are taught to smile, to placate, to take care of other people and not talk back. We are taught that if we do this well enough we may be safe from male violence. It's not true, of course, but that's the message. We've grown up with images of women "getting what they deserve." For being bitches and ballbreak-

ers and sluts. Being nice is a survival strategy for some of us. Others of us take our chances as "bad girls." Nice girls have to distance themselves from bad girls, though, and show the boys that they're "not that kind of girl." Or (we are told) they may be at risk too.

For lesbians, invisibility has been our safety and our trap. Being in the closet may be stifling, but it could save you from losing your job, your children, your life. It's frightening to leave that trap. When other lesbians do it, it can feel like they're endangering all of us, giving all of us a bad name. Sometimes we are quicker to punish each other than the outside world is.

Making lesbian sex art isn't safe. It's not invisible, and it's not always nice. Why does Kiss & Tell deliberately set out to do things that make a lot of people angry? Why did we walk into the middle of the porn wars when we could have been safe at home in bed? None of us loves conflict. Susan grew up in a conservative Christian family. She was punished for being a bad girl. Lizard learned to be silent before she even learned how to talk. Persimmon grew up with learning disabilities. She was punished for doing it wrong. We really just want to be good and quiet and do it right. We have such fine-honed fear. Why do we keep doing things that are bound to get us into trouble?

Coming together

KISS & TELL: The group that later evolved into Kiss & Tell started in 1984 as a big meeting of feminists who came together to talk about sexual representation—the whole "what is pornography, what is erotica" thing. It settled into a group of eight or so who met once a week. It turned out all of us were artists, which made sense, because as artists we had an extra stake in thinking about images. We were all artists and we were all confused. Our need to work through our confusion was the thing that held us together. It was bigger than anyone's need to show off how tough and cool she was, or how politically pure. We weren't pure, we were halfway desperate. It was time to stop pretending and look at where we really were.

She is vulnerable here, like me. Me, being called a prude by a boyfriend. Me, sitting in my mother's friend's gift shop minding the cash, reading Andrea Dworkin. Me, watching MTV recently and wanting to shoot the set, thankful that I usually just watch safe Canadian TV.

"We would probably really like each other if we met," I want to say to her, but already I can feel she is not listening either. She's made her statement.

Dee, who is co-ordinating all my activities in Halifax, steps into the pause and wraps it up. Applause, and then everyone files out. Some women stay to chat as I pick up my things. They're all busy doing courageous and fascinating projects, the way lesbians do. One of them just came out and is adding our book *Drawing the Line* to her library, "which already has 37 lesbian titles." One of them is doing her master's thesis on lesbian sexual imagery. One of them is making a video of herself and her lover fucking, recreating favourite movie scenes. Two of them have already made

We met for a couple of years. We had weekly updates on each other's sex and art lives. We each took hours telling our complete sexual histories. We learned to trust each other, to know that we could ask each other hard questions, to know that we could tell the truth and not be rejected.

We made art together. We had a "desire diary" that we passed around from week to week, where we each did collages about the current state of our sex lives. We made strange lingerie. Sometimes we would each start a piece of art about sex and give it to someone else in the group to work on, and someone else, and someone else, until we had all worked on each piece. Our group was a place where we could take chances, make art that frightened us, art that we sometimes decided to throw away and sometimes used as the basis for new directions in our individual art practices.

We never worked through our confusion, but we learned to stop pretending. We learned to make confused art. For a while, the group stopped meeting. Then a few years later, the porn wars were heating up and there was a lot of anger flying, and we again needed a place to ask hard questions and tell the truth. So we started up again, and eventually it was Lizard, Persimmon, and Susan, talking sex and making art.

SUSAN: My real reasons for turning up at that first meeting back in '84 didn't emerge right away. Like everyone else, I was confused. I had just finished several years of political work around issues of violence against women and I carried a secret that was aching to be told. It took a while, but I finally found the courage and safety I needed, within this group, to disclose the terrible truth: not only did I like looking at porn but I also made it.

At the same time as I was out there organizing Take Back the Night marches and leading discussions on the evils of pornography, I was leading a kind of double life in my studio, photographing my friends and myself in constructed scenarios that implied uninhibited and sexualized narratives of passion, lust,

their video and want to talk about outtakes—are ours as funny as theirs? This is the best part, I think. Somehow I doubt that straight artists get to meet so many incredible women.

But my cunt is elsewhere. It has noticed that She hasn't budged. She's tapping her copy of *Drawing the Line* absent-mindedly on her knee.

Watching.

Waiting.

Well, I can wait just as long as Her, I tell myself.

"Oh really?" I say to the master's student.

"Have you seen Deborah Bright's work?" I say to the video maker.

"Comedy lets people release sexual tension," I say to the other two.

Damn right I can wait just as long as Her. I look up and she's gone. Shit. I never could flirt right. Here I think we're building up some dynamic, and she just gets bored and leaves.

Maybe I imagined it.

I pack up. Dee turns out the lights. We head out the door to her car.

and betrayal. Images that I never showed. Images that would have disclosed another impossible truth, that I was queer.

Photographs have a wonderful ability to traverse the edge between what is commonly known as *reality* and *the invented*, making it unclear which is which. For myself and my friends these early images constructed themselves: we didn't know what we were doing or even why, we just knew that to make the pictures was to describe something that couldn't be put into words. Our pictures felt like proof that our reality could be altered, that the world we lived in and were part of was not the only world, and that within our imaginations dwelt another reality that was mysterious and potent.

For me this reality included the possibility of women together, and signified that beneath the outer trappings of our everyday masks and costumes there existed a body that hungered and thirsted for freedom. That beneath the artifice there existed another "self," another, more authentic body—in my case, a lesbian body that was struggling to name itself by imagining and then imaging its own unspeakable yearnings.

Those early representations were like canaries brought into a mine to test the toxicity of the environment, to see if it was fit for human use. If the photographs survived scrutiny, if the soft pseudo-lesbian content passed, then perhaps it would be possible to be what the pictures suggested one could be, to be a lesbian in the full sense of that word.

Looking at those pictures now, they don't seem to be saying much. They feel oddly out of place, yet it is in these images that the seeds of discontent took root and a means toward sexual liberation was first formulated. The magic and the power of representation rests in its ability to take the raw stuff of life, both conscious and unconscious, and shift meanings to create new ways of being in the world. Or so it seemed to me as I navigated the treacherous boundaries between the straight world I knew and the queer world I aspired to.

But I didn't imagine it, because here she is, outside. Sitting on a car, smoking a cigarette. Someone kisses her goodbye—the woman with the Butler decision question—and then she's alone, smoking.

"Come on," says Dee. "I'm parked over here."

But already I am making up some story about having left some stuff behind in the gallery office with Richard. "I'll, um, get a cab or take the bus," I say.

"You can't wait worth shit, " She says, and she's right this time. I feel like I am going to die if we don't fuck right now, here, on the street.

She takes a drag on her cigarette and looks at me.

"I've got some questions about censorship," she says.

"Sure," I say.

"I want to know how long you can keep talking about it when what you really want to do is fuck."

"It's an important issue," I say.

"Oh, I agree," she says with a grin. "Let's go for

Do

you hate my

bones?

coffee and discuss it."

Coffee? She wants to go for coffee? I'm ready to throw myself at her feet. Please, fuck me, I think.

"Fine. Coffee," I say.

We go to a coffee bar. Not a hip I-wish-this-was-a-warehouse-instead-of-a-storefront coffee bar, but an Italian one. There is a white fake marble fountain with peeing cupids, a pool table and video games. They know her in here, and they eye me. Meekly I let her order for me and follow her to the back where it's dark. We sit side by side against the wall.

"So tell me," she says.

"Tell you what?"

"How you ended up being anti-censorship when you used to be such an anti-porn activist."

I start the rap. I hear myself quoting from the talk.

"No, you. Tell me about you."

I start again. I don't know this woman, or do I? But she is looking at me intently, and I feel like she might understand instead of argue, so I tell her all

So it is with some irony that I realize that the first images I made of the lesbian body weren't of lesbians. They were fictions, designed to suggest a lesbian body. This point highlights another powerful and mischievous aspect of the photograph, its chameleon-like ability to suggest completely different things to different people. What is truth in the face of such a representation?

It wasn't until more than ten years later, in the decade in which I finally came out, that I was presented with the opportunity to make photographs with real live lesbian bodies, and it was as if a dam had burst open.

Between the lines

KISS & TELL: In 1988, we started work on what was to be our first collaborative work made for a public audience, DRAWING THE LINE. The catalyst for our project was a series of lesbian sex photographs by artist Li Yuen that were printed as an International Lesbian Week poster in Vancouver's gay, lesbian, and bisexual paper, *Angles*.[3]

3. *Angles,* September 1987.

This poster caused an uproar in our communities. *Angles* was flooded with letters, pro and con, for weeks after. There were organized meetings, spontaneous debates, contradictory commentaries:

"This doesn't represent my sexuality."

"How wonderful to see such a variety of lesbian sex."

"The pictures that are fragmented instead of showing the whole woman are implicitly violent."

"The fragmented shots are what you actually see when you're lying next to someone—the close up view."

"This one is so playful."

"This one is posed and stilted."

It was an amazing event in our community, because for the first time, the debate about imagery was focussed on a particular set of images, produced by and for lesbians, that had been widely viewed and circulated. We were looking at

the same pictures, and our reactions were incredibly diverse. One photo reminded a woman of the feeling of making love, when she could no longer tell whose body was whose, the feeling of dissolving into a tangle of arms, legs, mouths, moving together. The same photo reminded another woman of a picture she had once seen of a tangle of dead bodies.

Which woman was "right" about the meaning of the photo? Is it possible to honour both the one woman's joy and the other woman's fear? Is it possible to admit the mutability of images without retreating to a position that says all images are neutral?

Kiss & Tell decided to make a piece that would continue the exploration started in Li Yuen's work. DRAWING THE LINE is a series of 100 photographs, set literally within the context of the debate about sexual representation. Susan was the photographer and Lizard and Persimmon were the models. The overall concept and all decisions along the way were arrived at collectively. The photos cover a range of lesbian sexual practices, and are deliberately constructed to cover a range of problematic issues. At the exhibits, women viewers write their reactions directly on the walls around the photographs. Men write their comments in a book.

DRAWING THE LINE has been shown 16 times in 15 cities since 1988. The show still travels, and in every place women respond. Those polite and pristine gallery walls are soon scrawled over with writing. The photos float in a sea of text; not "fine art objects" but part of a loud, rowdy community argument and celebration. We want everyone to feel that they have a right to their reaction, and that they can speak out about it, even if it doesn't make perfect political sense, or upsets their best friend, or whatever. Some people write long, thoughtful analysis. Others react very directly and succinctly, saying things like "great," "stupid," "nice," "fuck me," etc. Viewers have their own dialogue with the anonymous commentators, and on it goes.

DRAWING THE LINE was created within a lesbian context that included re-

sorts of things, even things I hadn't thought of before and disagree with a sentence later. How it was, really, at those anti-porn slide shows and on those picket lines and later in bed with my lover who refused to picket . . .

She reaches across me for the ashtray, and her hand brushes my breast. I feel my nipple respond, and catch my breath.

"Don't stop," she says. "This is fascinating."

I can't tell if she's joking.

Her right hand is on my knee now. I can feel it

hot through my tights. It's not moving. With her left hand she is smoking. She is leaning forward, on her left elbow, watching me. I move one of my hands to touch her breast under her coat. She shrugs it away.

"Wait," she says.

I can't but I do. I go on talking about Red Hot Video.

"Tell me more about the slide shows."

"What about them?"

"Well, what did you like?" Her right hand is

sponsibility, collaboration, safety, community, and the wild, intoxicating freedom that came from uninhibited representation of our own lesbian bodies. We learned many things from this project, not the least of which was that the two bodies we represented over and over, Lizard's and Persimmon's, took on multiple and widely divergent meanings for other lesbians. No two responses to any single image were ever the same. Before long it became very clear that the notion of any single, unified account of what a lesbian body was or could be was an utter impossibility. The most we could do for our work was to provide it with a lesbian context. The "body" in that work was an untamed and unpredictable creature open to interpretation by whoever viewed it.

Truant virgins

PERSIMMON: In 1992, Kiss & Tell produced the multi-media performance and video TRUE INVERSIONS. It was a monster. It ate our lives for months. Three performers, one singer, four scenes, three video tapes, four audio tapes, and over 200 slides. And three technicians. At first Joelene Clarke was the only technician, and Suzo Hickey and Ali McIlwaine were just girlfriends who were going to come with us to Boston and Northampton for a romantic vacation. And maybe they would help out a little bit when we did our show. Ha! It was soon obvious that we couldn't do it without all three of them busting butt throughout the six-hour set-up, and then running the simultaneous tapes, slides, and lights during the show.

Girlfriends. Kiss & Tell is run on the exploited labour of girlfriends. Some of them don't think that's such a funny joke. The reason TRUE INVERSIONS has three videos (two used as background to other action, and one that plays by itself while we change costumes) is because one of my girlfriends, Lorna Boschman, is a video maker. We got the idea to make a two- or three-minute video segment and asked Lorna if she'd help us. She said yes. Then we gave her the script and she said "this is not a three-minute video." In the end it was 30 minutes. Oh well.

moving. Her fingers are on the inside of my knee, moving back and forth.

"Not everything. A lot of it was boring. And a lot of it was awful. Some of it made me want to cry."

"But what did you like?"

"Some of the images."

"What kinds?"

"What do you mean, what kinds? I liked some of the images, that's all."

"Well, did you like the lesbian images?"

"No. They weren't very realistic."

Her hand is moving up my thigh. Then it stops, moves away from my leg.

"Don't stop," she says, and pinches my nipple. Hard.

I gasp. "Can we go now?" I say.

"No," she says. "Wait. Talk." She takes a drag on her cigarette.

Her hand settles on my thigh again, higher than it was when it left. My skirt is being pushed up. It's hard to form the words now, but I do. I talk about the slides.

It was shot in two days, by Lorna's ace video crew along with a couple of re-inforcements from our side. Lorna had directed explicit sex scenes before and she was really comfortable, but some of the crew seemed to find it a little strange that my girlfriend was directing me having sex with Lizard. My other girlfriend brought us lunch. Life in Kiss & Tell.

And that was just the video. We still had to do four audio tapes, shoot the slides, build the set, etc. And we had to create a performance piece. Rehearsing, rewriting, reworking . . . We were still changing our script right up to the day of our first show. Actually, now that I think of it, we've changed our script on the day of every show we've ever done. Why would anyone want to be a perfor-mance artist? You can't ask for a week's extension if you're not ready to perform. You've got to be ready. You've got to get up and do it, and if you fuck up it's right out there in front of a whole bunch of people. Jesus. Why did I let them talk me into it? I hate it, I hate it, I hate it.

But I love the piece—I love the interwoven sex stories in the first section, where Susan and I have these mad back-and-forths building to a wild climax that Lizard grabs out of our hands. And then the part with Emily Faryna, the singer whose music is used in TRUE INVERSIONS, who eventually started per-forming live with us. Emily looking tough in a leather coat and pig snout, singing about surveillance, state control, and everyday working life. I can feel her voice rip through the audience while we're changing our clothes on stage be-hind her, and Ali up in the tech booth cruises us with a spotlight that moves like a police searchlight. And then the part where our slides are projected on top of a commercial porn video and they just float there like ghost images while fake les-bians have fake sex around, behind, and through them.

And I love sitting in the dressing room while the long video is on, gauging the audience by when they laugh, trying not to think of all the ways I could still blow it. And then we go back on for the part where we read letters to our moth-ers, explaining to them why we're doing this public sex thing. I have to stand up

"I liked the ones where the woman looked like she wanted it so bad she didn't care what happened. I liked the ones where they still had some clothes on. I liked the ones where they were doing it in public."

"I thought so," she says. It only takes one hand to smoke. The other one is moving up my thigh, closer and closer to my crotch. I am pinned by my desire, bunny in the headlights, butterfly on a pin. Please please come closer. I squirm to feel her hand on my cunt. She moves away.

"Wait." she says.

I can't wait. I can't. I can't. I can't.

"I've got to go to the bathroom," I say.

"I'll show you where it is." She puts her cigarette out, slowly, deliberately.

Meekly I follow her. I can hardly walk. I feel like everyone in the place is staring at me. How obvious is it that she is seducing me? Does she do this all the time? Do they know about how wet and tight and insane with lust I am?

The bathroom has no cubicles, it's just a room

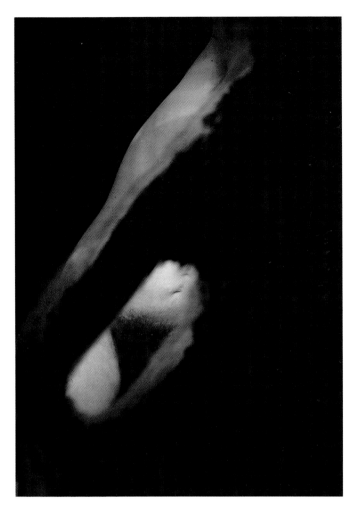

Married,

separated,

mother,

divorced,

single,

other?

with a door. She goes in and leans on the sink. She must have had a glove in her pocket. We pause, her eyes on me, my eyes on her hands, snapping the glove. When I close the door she reaches over me to lock it.

I grab her and kiss her.

I reach for her breasts and she pushes me away, but I am strong now. Nothing can stop me. I pinch them and bite them and suck them.

We are wrestling in the tiny room. I whisper to her, "Fuck me. Take me. Do anything. I'll do anything."

She is breathing hard.

She wants me.

"Let me fuck you," I say. She looks at me from a faraway place.

Everything stops.

Then I feel her hand on my mouth. Then I feel her hand in my cunt. I want to scream. That's why her hand is on my mouth, she knows everything, even my scream that she is taking away from the cold walls and putting in her eyes. She fucks me and I there alone on stage and talk to my mother about sex. Why did I let Susan talk me into this? How many people in the audience could possibly relate to growing up like me, in a left-wing family where your mother takes you on picket lines, and then in later years brags about your lesbian exploits to her friends? But it doesn't matter, I can feel the audience with me. I can feel them listening, and it's a rush like nothing else.

After that, it's easy—keeping count in my head in the dark so I can be there frozen when the spotlight hits—move—freeze—move. And Emily is doing Marlene Dietrich and I don't think about fucking up. I love that song.

KISS & TELL: Our first audience was a crowd of 400 lesbians at the York Theatre in Vancouver. To feel the excitement in that room was to understand the power of live theatre and its activist potential to move both performer and spectator in unexpected ways.

Informal lesbian performance occurs constantly, on the street, in the bars, and in our bedrooms. As lesbians we continuously perform for each other. It can be as simple as a discrete triangle worn at the ear, the cut of a jacket, a way of walking, or as flagrant as the live sex shows we organize in our bars. We are consummate actors. Some of us have been practicing stagecraft from our earliest years. We've learned to perform *lesbian* to find and attract each other and we've learned to perform *straight* when disguise is our best defense for survival.

Staging lesbian performance in a theatrical context implies theatre within theatre. The lesbian subject is performing herself performing herself. Taking our spontaneous theatre and putting it on a stage ritualizes and distances it, while at the same time acknowledging it, and, paradoxically, bringing it closer to home. Theatre offers a space where audience and artists can look each other square in the face. Whatever exchange happens does so immediately and irrevocably. There is power in this, not unlike the power people create when they consent to

fuck her and fuck her and fuck her screaming silently. We are pounding and sliding on the floor, and it is going to last forever.

When we have both come, I want to fall asleep. I could die happy. She dresses me, brushing my nipples again, touching my wet wet lips. I could start again.

"You'll have to wait," she says.

She stands up, unlocks the door, slips out, is gone.

sex. There is seduction, anticipation, desire, gratification (or not), intense sharing, and sometimes pain, sometimes love. A volatile and reactive mix.

Given the potential of live performance, the question becomes what would make it most effective as a tool for resistance? What strategies would be most useful for the spectator *and* the performer, to counter the oppressiveness of social rejection and political discrimination? How can we use theatre and performance to empower ourselves and tackle the contradictions in our lives? And how can we have *fun* while doing these things?

SUSAN: Theatre heals. It can also hurt.

4. "Lesbianville, USA," was the tag given Northampton, Massachusetts by the front-page story in that week's issue of the *National Enquirer*.

Standing on stage at the Academy of Music in Lesbianville, USA,[4] I noticed that several women walked out during part of our performance. Now this can be a very discouraging thing for a performer. An *"Oh no, that bad!"* type of feeling can quickly ensue, but I had a hunch that wasn't happening here. These women didn't go far, just to the front of the house, to the lobby. They stood in the open doorway, still listening, but they were smoking too and the outside exit was a comfortable distance away. The part of our show that prompted this mini-exodus wasn't the explicit sex, nor was it our experimentally formatted video. It was the letters we read aloud to our mothers.

Queer, lezzie, dyke, pervert, monster. I am your daughter, your beloved. I want you to know me—who I am, not what I am called.

It is hard to talk to you after so long. You were two years older than I am now when you died. The child I was then died with you, torn in two from grief. I dreamed you in a thousand dreams, and waking, your presence would linger like the scent of a forgotten perfume. How dare you leave me and turn out all the lights in your passing?

Now, you are back—here on stage, alive in memory, the recipient of this letter.

How will I explain myself to you, what sense would you make of this distance,

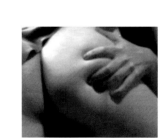

this difference? What sense would you make of this lesbian daughter, your own daughter, this unthinkable choice? How did we get from the ordered days of the family—clothespins, baking, church suppers, school meetings, regular appointments at the beauty parlor—to pornography, censorship, lesbian sex, and radical art? What strange path was it, from you to me, mother to daughter?

The word lesbian didn't exist in our world because lesbians didn't exist. The concept was unthinkable, impossible, unspeakable . . . repulsive. Yet the sheer weight of that silence was not enough to extinguish imagination. Friendships. Deep, passionate, engrossing friendships between women. I followed your example in this. I thrived in the love of friendship—and I crossed the line. The line that had no description, no form, no word—the line that separates our worlds—the line that gave me my name—lesbian.

—SUSAN (from TRUE INVERSIONS)

It made sense that some of our audience could have been affected by these letters, since we had been, too. When the idea first came up, when we realized that this was indeed an idea we could explore, an idea that stuck in the gut, it was initially greeted with absolute silence. For me the word "abject" suddenly took on the force of meaning. Miserable and wretched, it means, and so I felt as I attempted to bring my mother into our work. Lesbian sex and mom didn't quite fit, or else they did fit in ways that were impossibly confusing and painful. Each of our stories about our relationship with our mother was very different, yet the anxiety and grief and coming to terms with the past were things we shared.

There is the temptation to generalize, to try to figure out if there is a universal lesbian/mother experience, but I suspect this would be a mistake. There are far too many variables, too many stories, too many different ways of being. I can only speak for myself and I know that I have the need to discover some kind of coherency in this pain and to give it broader meaning.

I grew up with a societal understanding of what a mother is, of her precise

EDMONTON

I saw Her again in a bar in Edmonton.

I was there with a strange mix of university students, granola dykes, and leather girls who were looking after Kiss & Tell while we were in town. The bar was mostly men, mostly in couples, loud juke box, small dance floor. It was a quiet night, but every night was a quiet night. I didn't care. If we had been in Vancouver, everyone would have been complaining—what a dead night, this is boring, let's go to the Shaggy, Ms. T's, anywhere else but here. If we were in Vancouver the butch bottom in the chainlink vest wouldn't have been caught dead dancing with the scrub-cheeked grad student, laughing and bouncing up and down to the music, so uncool. But this was Edmonton.

It was a Euro crowd, with the exception of a tall thin East Asian fag who danced like a performance

location and function within this system called the family, within a culture that privileges heterosexually prescribed roles for women to the exclusion of any alternative choices. If a woman's self-definition is formed by a role, if her very existence is defined by that role, what possible relationship is she likely to have with a daughter who rejects that role for the risk and freedom of a lesbian alternative? For many lesbians the mother-daughter relationship is characterized by painful rejection and separation that is culturally reinforced by discrimination and rage wherever we turn.

It is one of those things some of us have a hard time talking about. Our silences speak volumes.

LIZARD: I have nightmares. There is one where we have forgotten our costumes for the second part and are fighting in the dressing room, about whether to go home and get them or to go ahead in the wrong outfits. Or the dream where Persimmon chats with her friends in the audience while the video is showing, and forgets her cue. Or the real life nightmare when we stood on stage realizing a prop was missing, Susan and I watching slack-jawed as Persimmon improvised.

Dreams are important. The first sex story I ever wrote was for TRUE INVERSIONS, and it came to me in a dream. All I had to do was describe it. I was paralyzed by fiction writing (of any kind, and especially sex stories), went to bed knowing I was going to miss *another* Kiss & Tell deadline, and woke up with a story. Phew.

Looking back on it now I realize that our minds have their own ways of circumventing our fears. It is really scary to write a sex story, because if no one else likes it it feels like a personal blow. Essays can be good or bad, clear or unclear, without a lot of personal pain, but if you try to write something that turns you on, and everyone else hates it, what does that say about you? Even in Kiss & Tell it can feel like your desires are weird.

artist, and a South Asian dyke professor with long black hair and an English accent who was sitting across the table from me.

I was talking to a femme who seemed to belong to the dancing chainlink butch (or vice versa, more likely). She was fat and smart and knew all about local politics. She kept a casual eye on the dance floor, not like she needed to worry about any sweet-faced academic, but more like she was enjoying the view.

"Three gay bashings in one day," she was saying. "That's what lesbian and gay visibility means in Alberta."

The dyke professor leaned across to us.

"And it's no wonder, with the fine example our government sets. First they say gays have more rights than anyone else, when we're not even covered by the human rights code! And now they're talking about restricting immigration—only English-speaking people need apply."

"Why do you stay?" I asked.

"We should just leave?" asked the femme. "We

But my story came to me unbidden, in a dream. It wasn't *my* story, really, so I could let them see it.

The other thing about my story is that it's pretty goofy. I mean, my life is pretty goofy, which is probably why that happened, but why a goofy sex story? (I can talk about this objectively because I didn't really write the story. It came to me in a dream, remember?) I think the goofiness works like the dream. It works like a spoonful of sugar. It works like a safety valve.

My story is all about a shy and nervous gal with a monster crush. She doesn't know how to come on to anybody in any kind of suave way. She's overwhelmed by lust. She makes a fool of herself. But she gets what she wants. You can laugh at her or with her. You can laugh because you've been there, or because you're anxious that Persimmon's character just slapped her girlfriend, or because Susan's character is turning you on, or because the images are from your fantasies, or because you've got some hot date with you, or your ex is in the next row, or whatever. You can laugh and it's a release and it's allowed. It brings you close.

I am convinced that people hear more through a joke than a lecture, and learn more from friends than enemies. However, I am also convinced that lying and pretending not to be angry do not serve the purposes of hearing or learning. This means that different audiences have profoundly different reactions to our show. Perhaps barriers are inevitable in political art-making. Maybe the difference is just that sometimes we erect the walls to enclose, instead of to divide. Sometimes we are united with our audience. Sometimes they feel like an adversary.

The pact between audience and performer is tenuous. When things don't work, it is brittle as ice. When things go well, it is steel cable, flexible and strong. It is sex without the contact, all images and words. Take me, says the audience, but do it right.

There are orgasms to be had.

should just give the province to the Aryan Nation?"

"And where would I go?" asked the professor. "To your fine province where feminist professors receive death threats and nothing is done about it?"

"Yes, but Alberta is . . . well, you know . . . everyone talks about it like it's worse," I offered lamely.

The professor sighed. "Perhaps it is. Or maybe it's just a convenient place for the rest of the country to feel superior to."

She took a swig of her beer. I took a swig of my mineral water. We contemplated Alberta. The bar was starting to fill by now and the air was thick with smoke. The chainlink butch stopped by our table long enough to give her girl a squeeze before going back to dancing. The music was still relentlessly middle of the road disco.

"Don't look now, but there's someone staring at you," said the femme.

"Me? Who? Where?"

"Over there at that table with all the flannel shirts."

The trick becomes how to weave this dynamic with the anger, pain, fear, and joy of our lives and politics. How to get the audience to figure it out along with us, to be right there, to talk beside us.

When I think about making a performance piece, I think about that old story about the Sun and the Wind. You know the one, where the Sun and Wind have a bet about who can get a man to take off his coat first. And the Wind tries to blow it off, and the man just clutches his coat tighter. But the Sun makes it so hot that the man takes off his coat himself.

That's what we are trying to do, make it so hot that you take off your coat yourself.

DOING IT TOGETHER: LESBIANS COLLABORATE

It is no coincidence that so much contemporary Canadian lesbian artwork is collaborative. The double marginalization of gender and sexual orientation makes voicing our positions difficult, and indeed dangerous. Do I have a right to speak? What is my language? How much abuse will I incur for being "too visible"?

—SHAWNA DEMPSEY[1]

Genius art

PERSIMMON: There's this cliché about Committee Art. Like everyone knows that great art can only be made by one individual Genius Art Star who doesn't bow to public opinion, political fashions, or anyone else's ideas. Unfettered and free, he goes where no man has gone before, and he goes alone or else it doesn't count. Committee Art is dull and predictable. Any Genius Art Stars involved are pulled down to the lowest common denominator. All risky and innovative ideas are vetoed and mediocrity rules.

Where did this strange idea come from? Who is served by it?

It's a very European idea, dating from the Renaissance, when art started to be divided from (and exalted over) craft. Craft was practical, art was of the mind. Art belonged to the nobility, or the church, and eventually the rising mer-

1. Shawna Dempsey, performance artist; letter to the authors, January 1994.

chant class. It wasn't something that common people could afford. If they had art it was folk art, a very different thing.

Artists fought to be seen as not "mere craftsmen." In the shifting class system of the time, they wanted to be seen (and paid) as more than skilled manual labourers like weavers and ironworkers. They wanted to be part of the intellectual/professional class.

Class hierarchies developed within art, whereby the "master artist" "owned" the work of his assistants, apprentices, and servants, sometimes taking credit for a painting that he had barely touched. But his "touch" was what counted.

The cult of artistic genius was born.

LIZARD: The myth of the lonely artist in the garret, starving but visited by the muse, is not only untrue, it can be destructive. Artists don't work alone. Their ideas are a product of their time and place, formed as much by circumstance as by inspiration.

The concept of "art" and its attendant institutions feeds and is fed by (among other things): the idea that there is such a thing as universally good and bad taste; concepts of individual genius located in white men; monetary valuation of single art objects over art forms available to everyone, like community dances or quilts.

This is the art tradition that prevails in mainstream North American culture. We are taught to associate art with a certain class, race, gender, and sexual orientation. And we do. By and large we buy the myth of the lonely artist in the garret.

If not the garret, then the seedy apartment. There are variations, but the pattern is endlessly repeated: the bad boy, the drug addict, he's troubled, dangerous, not responsible for his actions because of that uncontrollable muse. For some reason these wildly original figures are all white men, preferrably quaintly misogynist. William Burroughs. Jim Morrison. Paul Gauguin. Sid Vicious. To name a few. Icons of Western European culture have built their careers on this

I looked. Then I looked again. It was Her. That Woman. The one who fucked me over (and over and over) in Halifax. And she was staring at me.

I looked away, confused. It couldn't be Her. She was three thousand miles away. And she looked different. Her hair was the wrong colour. Her face was the wrong shape. She was too thin. It had to be someone else.

But it was Halifax. I recognized the eyes, the angle of her head, the way she sat, arms crossed, legs spread.

The femme smirked. "Maybe she wants your autograph."

"No. I know her." I looked again. She was still staring.

"Oh god," I said.

"Is that 'oh god,' like we should scare her off, or 'oh god,' like we should gracefully fade and tell your friends you won't be back tonight?"

"I don't know! I thought I'd never see her again," I said.

The professor shook her head sadly. "Our friend

image, and many of them— like Pablo Picasso, Elvis Presley—have added barely disguised ripoffs of the art of people of colour to their individual "genius."

Working collaboratively flies right in the face of that. It acknowledges that much of the art in the world is made by people working together. It forces us to deal with our ideas in a new way—to challenge the notion of a universal aesthetic, and simultaneously explore our common values. It's a dynamic and fluid process.

Women who work collaboratively have to come to terms with each other's differences, but we also support each other. In a world where women's art is devalued, we can encourage each other to continue to create and to be visible. Written down, these sound like motherhood concepts—well-meaning but too nebulous to have practical implications for change. But they do have practical implications.

I joined an art collective because the format was familiar to me. At the time I had an abiding interest in art, and a smattering of art education. I did not/would not call myself an artist, because I didn't fit the image. I lived and worked in co-ops and collectives, inspired by constant discussion with other feminists, anarchists, unionists. Troubled by issues of sexual representation, it came naturally to me to find a group where I could work out this trouble. Why would I make an art piece by myself when I could sit down with other women and find out what they thought? The art pieces came later.

Feminist collaboration is part of a continuum. At one end are the lone geniuses. At the other end are groups like Kiss & Tell, where the art is frequently so collectively produced that even we cannot tell who did what. Right next door are the myriad women's art groups, where artists bring their art and issues for collective discussion. We and they rely on collaboration with the women's community, some of which comes in the form of technical assistance, or a garage to store things, or carpentry advice, or gallery sitting. Much of it is also feedback,

seems a bit incoherent. Perhaps she needs some help."

They pulled me out of my chair and shoved me toward the table where Halifax was sitting.

She looked good in a flannel shirt. Some girls do.

"Hi," I said.

She stared at me. So did the other women at her table. So much for prairie hospitality.

"Um, remember me?" Not a great opening line for an almost famous artist from the big city.

The women at the table looked away.

"I met you in Halifax?" my voice squeaked. I probably sounded desperate. I was making a fool of myself. Maybe it wasn't her.

But it was her. She glanced at me and looked away. The other women shifted nervously.

"Well uhh . . . see you around," I said, trying for nonchalance and failing. She was studying her thumbnail. She had lovely bitten cuticles. She was a jerk. Fuck her. I turned to go back to my table and caught the professor looking away, as if she hadn't

Stripped

of

history?

just watched me be humiliated by a table of flannel shirts, which of course she had. Damn. I walked out of the bar. It seemed like a good idea at the time.

It was late night downtown; empty streets, locked doors, stars rioting in the big Alberta sky. I crossed on a red light. Rebel rebel. Maybe I'd walk all night. Maybe I'd run into k. d. lang and she'd take me home. But she lives in Langley now, not Alberta. Maybe I'd get the bus back to my hotel room.

I heard footsteps, faint at first, about a block behind me. Hah! She *did* remember me. I wasn't going to turn around. No way. I could play hard to get too. I heard more footsteps. Did she bring all her flannel friends? Maybe it was just some lost tourists, looking for a midnight mall. I sped up a little. So did the footsteps. I looked over my shoulder, casual like. Their shaved heads gleamed under the street lights. Damn.

There were five or six of them, skinny white boys walking in a tight pack, their gangling adolescent

criticism, heated debate, letters to the editor. By the time the art is in its final form, whose is it?

PERSIMMON: Which brings us back to Committee Art. I've certainly been involved in collaborations that were as bad as that cliché, and worse. Ones where no one will say when they disagree with someone else for fear of hurting their feelings, or where everyone wants to do it her way and no one else's ideas are worth shit, or two people fight it out for control and everyone else cowers in the corner. If any art at all gets made in those circumstances, it's a miracle.

When collaboration really works, there's nothing more exhilarating. You challenge each other, support each other, push each other past your limits to places you never could have gotten to on your own. *I get an idea, which sends you off on a strange tangent, and then she sees the thing that will pull it all together.* I don't know why it works with some people and not with others. It's not from having the same philosophy of art or the same working style or the same politics. It's like falling in love, you can't predict it and you can't control it. Or at least I can't.

One of the best collaborations I was ever part of was with a woman who wasn't an artist, didn't like artists (too fancy), never went to art galleries, and was in the process of breaking up with me—the most prolonged and miserable break-up either of us had ever been through, during which we made an art show together (screaming at each other as we hung the show, scaring the gallery girls). Afterward, we agreed that it had been absolutely worth it and we never wanted to go through anything like that ever again.

Which, now that I think about it, is what Lizard and Susan and I say about the year we did TRUE INVERSIONS. Is there a lesson here that I'm not learning? But Susan and Lizard don't scream under stress—they get all quiet and tight and I scream.

There are endless styles of collaboration. Sometimes everyone does every-

grace transformed to a threat on this dark street. I sped up. The skinheads sped up. I crossed the street. They crossed after me. There wasn't an open store on the whole block. Fuck Edmonton on a Saturday night. I turned the corner and someone grabbed me.

"Come on!" she whispered and pulled me into a run, down the block and into an alley. The boys were out of sight around the corner, but I could hear them shouting and running after us. Without hesitating she leaped onto a parked car,

clambered up a ladder of steel rungs conveniently set into the side of the building, onto the flat roof, and out of sight.

"Gee, she must really know Edmonton," I thought as I flung myself after Her.

When I reached the roof, I tripped over her in the darkness and she pulled me down on top of her.

"Ssshhhh," she hissed.

Down below I could hear the skinheads reach the end of the alley and fade away. I was suddenly

thing equally, but there's nothing that says you can't use your individual strengths to the max. On our first DRAWING THE LINE shoot we all took turns behind the camera, but since Susan's been a photographer for 20 years, it was no big surprise that her photographs were way more skillful. Lizard and I were more excited about taking on the challenges of modelling than the prospect of learning photography. So on the shoots and in the darkroom we had our individual roles, while the concept, decision making, and ongoing ideas happened among all of us.

But in the eyes of some people, that made Susan "the artist" and Lizard and I were "just models," an old and venerable class hierarchy of the art world. Collaboration is very cutting edge and groovy these days, but it's strange how many critics and editors and arts administrators still don't seem to get it. The idea of an artwork "belonging" to an individual artist is hard to get rid of. It's kind of like when you're non-monogamous and everyone wants to know which one's your "real" girlfriend.

Susan was the one who bore the brunt of that failure of understanding. It's bad enough having your part in making something ignored, but getting public credit for work your friends did is even worse. She didn't want to be separated from us like that. She didn't want to steal our credit, but they kept shoving it at her. She would explain it patiently to interviewers, curators, and publicists, and then feel responsible when her name was the only one mentioned.

TRUE INVERSIONS made it more complicated, if nothing else. Sometimes it's written up like I'm the director (no way!) and no one else is mentioned. Other times it's Susan's and my show and Lizard disappears. Or Lizard gets credited with writing everything. So we fire off a form letter (you know it's bad when you have a form letter to defend invisible collaborators) and try not to resent whoever is Star for the Day.

acutely aware of my position and rolled off of her. This put me a little too close to the edge of the roof, but it seemed safer, somehow, than lying on top of Her.

"They're gone," I whispered.

"For now."

We lay there, listening. The dark silhouettes of other buildings rose around us and the stars burned overhead. The roof smelled of tarpaper and prairie air. Halifax moved closer, running her hand along my arm. I could smell her. I remembered how she had touched me in that coffeebar washroom. I remembered how abruptly she had left.

"No," I said. Her hand hesitated.

"We have to talk," I said.

"Okay," she said. "What do you want to talk about?"

"What do I want to talk about?" I sat up. It's a better position for indignation. "Well, let's start with where did you go? Why did you just disappear? Who the hell are you, anyway? And what the fuck are you doing *here*?"

Glass houses

SUSAN: Although DRAWING THE LINE was a collaborative project, because it is photography, a hierarchy is consistently assumed. Camera equals control; model equals passivity. The medium implies an inherent power relationship that is very difficult to lose, despite the fact that we consistently exposed our process as a collaboration. The common assumption is that the person who runs the medium controls the representation. While we were able to deconstruct this process in our art making, what was true was that I, as the photographer, had one very distinct advantage: I produced sexual images of other women but my body was safely hidden behind the camera. Didn't this reinforce the very power structure we were attempting to dismantle?

In Kiss & Tell's second work, TRUE INVERSIONS I was able to have the sometimes terrifying experience of being the subject of the camera's gaze. This was a very valuable experience because many aspects of the subject position, such as the raw vulnerability and the sense that some sacred part of the self has been removed, can only be gleaned from experience. Loss of control was balanced with feelings of power, recognition, and excitement about the art-making process.

Without sensitivity the very act of *taking* a picture or *shooting* a scene can sometimes border dangerously on abuse. Many women can recall very harrowing encounters with photography, ranging from childhood abuse and coercive studio sessions to finding images of themselves displayed in exhibits or published without their knowledge or consent.

I remember clearly the process Lizard and Persimmon engaged in, as we created DRAWING THE LINE, to come to a place of acceptance in themselves, that yes, they would really allow these images of their bodies to be made public. Their incredible willingness to take risks that allowed this work to exist. I was sympathetic, encouraging, and understanding about the difficulties, yet I never really got it until I did it.

"Saving your ass," she said sweetly.

That stopped me. I had forgotten to be grateful. Damn. I was trying to stutter out my thanks when she lunged at me and pulled me down beside her, her hand over my mouth. I kicked at her and tried to squirm out of her grip, but she held me.

Then I froze. I could hear the soft footfalls in the alley below, the half-whispered words of the skinheads. There was a sudden clang of metal on metal. A cat screamed. Then silence.

Her body was warm next to mine. I pressed against her.

"Shit," I whispered.

"Ssshhh," she replied, her hot breath in my ear.

The skinheads were whispering again, closer, then further away. I could follow their voices as they moved methodically from one end of the alley to the other, searching. She held me close, one hand moving down my back, searching. I pushed it away. She stopped. My ass felt cold where her hand had been. I put it back, and felt silent laughter on my cheek.

Not that any of us fights the same demons—our fears are as specific as our strengths, yet there is something about putting your body on the line in a representation that has its own unique qualities. Going public with a work is just that, public. Public means everybody that wants to, gets to see the work. This might include family members, the parents of your child's friends, teachers, classmates in school, your own students, the guys at work, your colleagues, as well as every friend in your phone book. It can be daunting. The actual making of the work is fun and exciting and creative—what is terrifying is the question what will people think? How will they judge me, weigh me, measure me? Having worked to overcome the prohibitions and inhibitions so deeply rooted in myself, what will this mean to the people who know me? How will this work activate the prohibitions in them and how will they react?

Sex for art

PERSIMMON: I remember the first time I ever kissed Lizard. It felt so strange. I knew her so well and so little. We had met together for so long, sharing the down-and-dirty details of our sex lives, but we had never gone out for coffee, met each other's girlfriends, been in a room alone together. We never saw each other outside of Kiss & Tell meetings. And then at one of those meetings we kissed. I touched her breasts. She grabbed my shirt and pulled me tight against her body. And Susan took photographs. Weird.

We all took turns being behind the camera that first night, so I kissed Susan too, but that was different. That was like practicing kissing with my sister when we were in grade school—awkward, uncomfortable, hilarious. But doing it with Lizard was hot.

I didn't expect it. I hadn't been aware of being attracted to Lizard—hell, I *wasn't* attracted to Lizard. She wasn't someone I would fall in love with, or have a secret crush on, or try to pick up in a bar. But when we started doing it, there was this spark . . .

The boys were getting louder, laughing at jokes I couldn't hear. The occasional word floated up from the alley—screw, bitch, kill. She kissed my throat, my eyes, my mouth, pausing to undo a few buttons, and a few more. The night air licked my breasts. Her hands were hot and hard on my hard nipples. The skinheads were yelling. I was moaning, muffling my mouth in her neck, tasting her salt skin.

There was a loud crash below, then another.

"Garbage cans," she breathed into my ear.

"They're trashing the alley."

In my mind's eye I could see the sounds, cans kicked, rolling away, spilling garbage. Her arms were around me, silent, defiant. Her smell filled me. I clung to her, biting her neck, her lips, rocking against her blue-jeaned cunt. She held me, open, yearning. Her hands slow, deliberate, undeniable, on my thighs. Her mouth. Her hips. She undid me, found me, wet and desperate. The sound of breaking glass, store windows, car windows. My cunt was huge, swollen. It filled the sky. Her slow

Name

my

differences

strokes filled me, forced me open, open, holding
me gasping on the edge of helpless powerful
breaking like glass falling the stars screaming
silence breaking, my fingers twisted in her
flannel shirt.

It didn't change anything. Or if it did, it was in subtle, underground ways. I didn't suddenly start to yearn after her, or feel shy around her, or want to buy a wedding ring. It was what it was. Susan behind the camera was as much a part of the sexual dynamic as Lizard and I—sometimes turned on, sometimes nervous, sometimes plain practical. It quickly became comfortable—a relationship I could trust, women I could risk myself with.

LIZARD: When we first started doing the shoots for DRAWING THE LINE, I had had sex with a grand total of three women in my whole life. I didn't have any idea what I looked like when I was fucking (not many people do), and I had no idea whether what I was used to doing in bed was "normal" or not. I had/have a lot of self-consciousness about my sexuality and what I like.

Doing those shoots was a revelation. It was such great therapy for me that for a while I felt quite evangelistic about being a sex model. First, I got to have sex that was clearly defined beforehand. In the early shoots we outlined everything before we started. And I mean everything. "In this shoot we will touch breasts but not genitals," we'd say. Or, "We'll kiss and grope but our clothes will stay on." I probably wouldn't want to have sex with my lover that way, but in the shoots I had space to look at each thing, and how I felt about it, separately, without worrying about its emotional impact on someone else.

Another thing was that eventually I got to try out many different practices and scenarios. I could try out a fantasy situation and discover I didn't find it that hot! Or that something I had always thought would be boring is a thrill to do.

I know that ideally we all feel free to experiment like this in our everyday lives, but in my experience this is not often the case. Relationships enhance sex, but can also intrude on it. A sex shoot is nothing like sex—it stops and starts, and is often uncomfortable. But modelling in sex photos does isolate some parts of sexual practice from others, and I have found this personally very gratifying.

Okay, so that's what it was like *doing* the pictures, but what about after, when they're up in a gallery?

Photography and video (and probably film, but we've never done that) are distant media. Distant, that is, in that the experience of the shoot is a long way from the final product. In my work with Kiss & Tell I have always seen the pictures about ten times before anyone outside the group sees them. I can veto anything at any time. And what the photos look like often bears no relation to what I felt like while modelling for them. All this distance has always made me feel safe about our photos and our videos. Performance is a lot scarier because it is so immediate.

My reaction to seeing the first Kiss & Tell prints was relief. Relief because they looked like sex pictures to me. I couldn't believe that I, me, Lizard Jones, actually looked like someone being sexual. No one was saying that my pose was weird or anything. This is an affirmation that has stayed with me. My way of fucking is okay! Every woman should hear this at least once.

Now these images have been more places than I can even imagine. I feel increasingly distant from the woman in those images, which is probably a lucky thing. Sometimes my picture looks up at me unexpectedly, illustrating a magazine article I've never even heard about.

Strangers want to talk to me about it, and I don't always feel safe. The distance of the medium comes back to haunt me. I realize the pictures are out in the world in myriad contexts I can never control. There is no turning back, taking a break, stopping for a breather to reconsider.

I live in a culture where image is currency, and this is not something I considered before embarking on these projects. I read about fashion models with new interest now. One "super model" (that's what they call them) described her paranoia when on cocaine: "Suddenly I'd think that there were 5,000 people standing around me trying to take my picture." What does it mean that I have become so comfortable being sexual in front of strangers? That kind of paranoia

SYDNEY

The music is blasting so hard it is bruising the soles of my feet. It is crashing through the courseways of my veins, trailing along the red blood into every limb, every nerve straining, pulsing with the beat of this maddeningly sweet music. I close the shutters of my mind down to a single sensation.

This vibrating, swinging floor beneath my feet.

To hear, to feel, but not to see. To open my eyes and look is to enter into the dizzy spectacle that is Sydney's Gay & Lesbian Mardi Gras. To lose myself once again in that riot of colour, pageant and movement, Australia's answer to Gay Pride. Drag queens galore, leather dykes, queer extraterrestrials. Twenty thousand queers crammed into one throbbing venue, one wildly perverse womb, on this sweltering hot February night. It is enough to shut my eyes and see through other senses.

can overcome me in bed with my lover. I do things that come naturally to me, but I practiced them while shooting the video, because they look good. Suddenly the camera is in bed with us, too. It is hard to separate the image and the person.

Kiss & Tell has tried to combat the traditional model/camera relationship by giving Persimmon and me control over our images. As the visible women in DRAWING THE LINE, we had more power than Susan in some ways, and more vulnerability in others. When it came time to do TRUE INVERSIONS, the two of us had a wealth of experience to draw on, while Sue was starting from scratch. We had called ourselves performers in the DRAWING THE LINE pictures, and could move to live and video performance from there. We knew what we looked like!

Persimmon and I also had a well-established sex-shoot relationship. Both of us noticed how different, how much more difficult it was to do the sex scenes with Sue. After four years of touching Persimmon on camera, I had come to anticipate certain things. I was surprised to realize this. As our video director Lorna Boschman put it, we have a "long-term non-relationship."

Who we aren't

LIZARD: Kiss & Tell does not represent all lesbians. Three women couldn't possibly do that, and it would be arrogant to try. Instead, we lay our own bodies on the line as models and performers. We try to make the particular—of our own process and politics—as evident as the general. However.

For some women who see our work, even though it's an entire room or an entire evening of lesbian pictures, they may come away from it feeling "Oh no, excluded again." We are all three white and able bodied. None of us is fat. I am in my thirties and Persimmon and Susan are in their forties. Many, many women aren't represented by our three bodies.

Lesbians of any kind are virtually invisible in mainstream culture. This absence of representation puts pressure on the pictures that are there. Sometimes

So it is that I *feel* her before I see her. Not an actual touch, just a sensation that someone is there. Disconcerting and real enough to make me open my eyes. I'm surrounded by the chaos of hundreds of moving bodies, lights flashing and rippling.

Everything moves but Her. She is about ten feet away, standing completely still and looking at me with astonishing intensity.

In the first breath I take in her eyes. Clear grey and compelling. In the next moment I see her

mask, all feathers and ribbon and bits of leather, like some kind of mythical punk bird. She's tall and wearing very little. Her body is painted or tattooed in swirling patterns of intricate design, part Celtic princess, part Hell's Angel.

Why the fuck is she staring at me like that? I begin to walk toward her. My eyes never once leave hers. When I get close I start to ask her but she lightly places two fingers on my lips. Then she signs something but I don't know what it means. She laughs. As she shakes her head I can just hear

there is an expectation that they represent everybody. In a show like DRAWING THE LINE, the simple fact there there are *so many* photos makes it hard to avoid that expectation. This is the context of our work, and we may acknowledge it, but that doesn't change the situation.

We live in a society where it's considered "normal" to be able bodied. Thin, white adults are assumed to be the "standard" that difference is measured against. These assumptions are very strong, stronger than any disclaimer we put in our artists' statement. We may say, "Look, it's just us, and there are lots of other kinds of lesbians." But the unspoken messages of this culture drown us out.

Given how the world has been taught to look at white thin female nudes, can an image of me escape being seen as "normal"? How can I call it into question? One way is to support the production of as wide a range of images as possible, so that there is no way one of them can be seen as generic. Another way is to make images that are as particular as possible, to keep reminding people that this is not Lesbian, it is Lizard Jones, 32-year-old middle-class closet case.

I don't think these ways of working are mutually exclusive. In fact, I think they have to go together in order for either one to work. As lesbian artists, we have to be as clear as possible about where we are coming from, and as particular as possible about our own experiences and opinions. As cultural activists, we have to work to increase the visibility of all kinds of lesbian artists, and all kinds of particular experiences.

These are my goals, but the reality remains difficult, and frequently confusing. No one comes to an art show or a performance without assumptions, and sometimes no amount of particularity on our part can shake them. When we are specific, this usually means talking about one thing at the expense of something else. In the process, what do we assume about what is left unsaid? Some unspoken things are always, and sometimes erroneously, presumed to be present. Others are erroneously presumed absent.

the music from tiny bells that are woven into her dark hair.

This woman is achingly familiar to me. I want to touch her. But I *don't* know her. I know nothing about her. She signs again and begins to move to a rhythm of her own invention. It's *almost* like dancing. I'm drawn to move with her. I feel really awkward. Tuning out the sounds of the party helps.

We dance for a long time. The noise of the carnival becomes fainter and fainter. My attention is riveted. I can't shake the feeling that I know her. I want to see her face.

Her eyes are locked on mine. She stomps the ground, I stomp the ground. I lift my arms up, she does too. Like children playing at mirrors we follow each other. Mimicry. We act like clowns, and start laughing. We're animals, prowling and stalking our prey. Hunter and hunted locked in some deadly game of survival. I move in close, she backs away.

Her skin is glistening with sweat and the bright feathers of her mask are cascading over her naked shoulders.

These problems aren't resolved in any one piece of work. These are problems that are starting to be addressed as more and more people demand representation beyond stereotypes and access to the means of representing themselves. These are problems that are starting to be addressed as artists with relative privilege are challenged to examine their assumptions and share their access to power.

SUSAN: I have to watch myself. My impulse to speak for others. To speak a reality not my own. This comes from a caring place, but that doesn't redeem it.

Sometimes it is wishful thinking. Like maybe we are a unified group, we queers. At the very least we should act like it so we can get political leverage and appear to the heterosexual majority as though we have clout. They don't need to know our internal divisions and factions.

Then I remember what it felt like those times when someone spoke for me. The gratitude (maybe), the fear that they wouldn't get it right, the desire to speak for myself (too dangerous), and finally the settling for second best (safety through silence).

There are fierce expectations when a minority voice does get heard. The incredible responsibility of those who speak out—that they get it right—that all the silences be broken by that single voice.

Knowing the impossibility of this doesn't alleviate the need, the hurt, the oppressive silence itself.

Until all voices are heard no voice will be free of this contradiction.

Power lines

SUSAN: Collaboration isn't always easy. Women artists have to fight and push for every bit of ground they can claim in the high-stakes game of recognition, support, and success in what is commonly called "the art world." For lesbian

artists this slice of pie is smaller yet, with even more shut doors, glass ceilings, and heterosexist barriers. Collaborating with other women or other lesbians can seem very threatening, like a give-away of hard-earned ideas, resources, talents. It can seem unfair, as if giving away these things means to only get partial credit, a third or a fourth or even a fifth of the attribution we feel we deserve.

In this culture, collective art practice is associated with loss of control, power, and material reward. This conception is completely reinforced by art institutions and funding bodies, artists' fees and grants. Awards, which maintain one artist at poverty-level wages, stay the same regardless of the number of people involved in the production. What used to pay one month's rent now pays for a week.

The material condition—sometimes referred to as poverty—of being a lesbian artist involved in collaborative work is an example of the type of issue we have had to address and deal with as part of our collective process. In Kiss & Tell we have different class backgrounds, although our current bank accounts are about the same, which is to say precariously unstable. This matter of different backgrounds plays itself out in curious ways and provides an example of how power issues can be obvious and dealt with directly, or elusive, hidden, and potentially destructive.

I grew up in a small town in rural USA where everybody was about the same, which is to say poor. A good education meant not getting pregnant by grade 12 and having a passable sense of the three R's, reading, writing and 'rithmetic. A lot of water has gone under the bridge since those small-town days, including a university degree (which was finally achieved at the age of 41), yet this background, this lack of a good childhood education, has had a profound impact on my self-esteem and how I have felt on occasion within my collective.

For example, when we are asked to do radio interviews as a group, we always agree to do them, but for a long time I felt a sickening dread at the prospect of these interviews, because I realized that the more I did them the worse it got.

Born

a woman?

I want to see her face.

The light takes on a reddish hue. We are slowing down.

Her hands are on her body. Stroking her body. I'm really hot. I start to undo my clothing as she looks at me. As I drop my skirt on the ground a small cloud of fine red dust rises up and settles on my sweat-drenched skin. She's streaked with red dust too. Her hands run patterns through these stripes, swirls and eddies of skin and sand.

Slowly she caresses herself. Her hands are sliding over her smooth skin. I do the same thing, as if we are still playing the game but I'm feeling something else. It's *her* hands I want on my skin. But I only have my own touch and it feels like liquid fire as I watch her watch me.

She's teasing me. Holding out her breasts, lascivious witch. Now turning quickly and grinding her hips. Slowly in one direction and then the other. I can feel my desire rising. I want to touch her and to be touched by her. Desperately. But I can't move. I'm spellbound. This game is devilish.

"It" was my increasing tendency to be silent, to lose my ability for speech in the face of this pressure, this cross-examination of our work on live radio, and ironically it became worse when I was with Persimmon and Lizard.

"It" was a class issue. I felt that Lizard and Persimmon were more articulate, better able to discuss our ideas and our work. Their seeming lack of nervousness, their ability to talk easily to the media, the speed of their responses to questions, their verbal skills seemed far superior to my own. I started digging a hole and whenever we did a talk or an interview and these feelings of "not being as good as" popped up, to this hole I retreated, silent and safe.

Fortunately for me, I wasn't there too long before the problem was identified and discussed and named by all of us. With practice on my part and sensitivity on theirs, this is no longer an issue for us and I enjoy doing radio interviews as much as they do.

Class issues also come up in discussions about artists' fees, whether or not we require them, if so how much, what is our bottom line, and so on. I have often found myself in opposition to both Lizard and Persimmon on these issues, in ways that aren't obviously class-related at first glance. Recognizing that this anxiety, stress, and opposition *is* part of a dynamic of class difference helps make sense of it. It is incumbent on all of us to think about and change our attitudes and habits when faced with these differences. Our commitment to making sense of difficult issues is one of the things that keeps us together.

Unaddressed, a power imbalance that is acutely felt by one member and unnoticed by others has the potential to fracture a collective. Within Kiss & Tell, each of us has been alone on the losing end of a power imbalance more than once. Negotiating power, attempting to understand how it works, learning to give it up when necessary or to take it on when needed, analyzing state power, empowering ourselves through our work—these issues of power are constant threads in our lives and in our collaborations.

She kneels on the ground, legs apart. I crouch down in front of her. Her lips are slightly open and I can feel the draw of her ragged breath. There is the scent of eucalyptus as she reaches out her arms, palms extended, and begins to trace the curves of my body. Her hands are inches away.

Tenderly she fondles me but she doesn't touch me. Sensitive fingers articulate every mound and valley of my body, no crease too small for her inquisitive probing. It is torture. The nearby passage of her hands electrifies my flesh. I'm past endurance, and I'm helpless to respond.

When she reaches my breasts she kneads and teases the air in front of my nipples. They jump erect as if to reach of their own accord for her touch. She merely laughs and leaves them wanting as she continues her wanderings.

The heat is bearing down on me, choking my breath. As hot as the fire inside my body, which she stokes with each passing moment.

Her face is near my cunt. Her silvery tongue is lapping and circling the air about its entrance.

This is one of the challenges of collaborative work and one of its great strengths. In this process of grappling with power relations rests the means of transforming them, both at a personal level, and socially and politically. Collaboration is an alternative and highly resistant model of creative interaction. It is a process that demonstrates a method of art making which can be democratic, transformative, and empowering, and which has the potential to renew and build community.

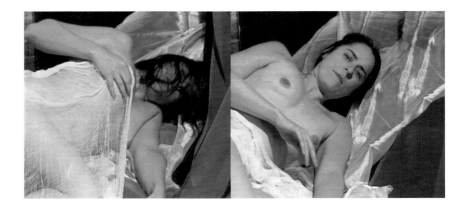

REDEMPTION AND TRANSGRESSION

Identity is what you can say you are according to what they say you can be.

—JILL JOHNSTON, 1973[1]

I'm not sure I like having my sexuality touted as a fad. It makes me feel exposed and grouchy. I resent having my sexuality processed, packaged, and fed back to me in the name of fashion. I'm a pervert, not a trend.

—LILY BURANA, 1993[2]

Sex and/or love

PERSIMMON: Sex is redeemed by love. Our liberal straight friends defend us by saying if two people really love each other, what does it matter if they're two women instead of a man and a woman. Lesbianism is no different from heterosexuality. Love makes it all okay.

Love is terrific, but does our sex really need to be redeemed? It's a view with roots in certain branches of Christianity. Sex is dirty and bad and belongs to the devil, unless it's blessed by God in holy matrimony and then it's pure and transcendent, a sacrament of love.

Lesbians fighting for custody of their children, or job benefits, or immigra-

1. Jill Johnston, from Celia Kitzinger, "Liberal Humanism as an Ideology of Social Control: The Regulation of Lesbian Desire," in *Texts of Identity*, ed. John Shotter, Kenneth J. Gergen (London: Sage Publications, 1989), 82.

2. Lily Burana, "I Did Madonna," *Taste of Latex* 9 (1993): 47.

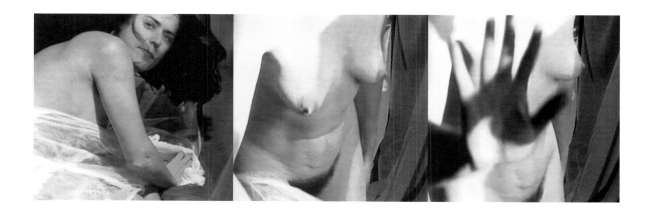

tion rights, or just for the tolerance of their neighbours, use the love defense over and over. "We love each other," we say, "we're just like you." Just like straight people, just like white people, just like gentiles, just like *Leave it to Beaver*. It's a way to be understandable, non-threatening to a society with narrow rules of social acceptability.

Sometimes we have to use that defense to survive. Sometimes we forget that it's just a defense and we internalize it. But do we really want to fit this narrow society? Love doesn't make lesbian sex okay. Lesbian sex *is* okay. Sometimes we need to stand up and say, "Get used to it."

If our sexuality needs to be redeemed, so do pictures of our sexuality. Sex pictures are redeemed by art. Art is sacred. Art transforms smut into erotica. Even in Canadian law, where porn is banned because it is believed to *cause harm*, artistic merit saves it. So if it's art it's okay, even though it (supposedly) hurts people? The logic of anti-porn laws eludes me, as usual.

Historically "erotic art" has meant rich men's sex pictures and "pornography" has meant poor men's sex pictures. The legal defense of artistic merit protects work with high production values and high art aspirations—art that takes more money to produce and is aimed at a well-educated market. It's a class distinction. The law is set up so that we can use our art school diplomas to buy us protection that sex workers have no access to.

Sex is also redeemed by intellectual seriousness. In Kiss & Tell we fall for that one too, sometimes. Sometimes when we're up in front of a mostly straight or mostly hostile audience, we find ourselves acting like our work isn't about sex. We talk on and on about the politics of censorship, or the postmodern discourse of identity and representation, or something equally serious and important. It's *so* much more respectable than making sex pictures. And it's true we're *totally obsessed* with censorship and representation and we love to talk about those things. But we're also kind of interested in actual sex, too. So now you know.

I imagine her sharp white teeth. I want their bite.

I'm soaking wet. My thirst for her is unbearable.

She is coming closer and closer. I can feel her hot breath cooling the pulse of my quivering lips. She backs off slightly and raises her hand within my view. She's signing again and this time her meaning is unmistakable.

One finger, two fingers, three fingers she thrusts into the air.

Touch me.

Over and over, matching the beats of my heart,

she draws her sign. I can feel the muscles of my vagina take up her steady rhythm. I don't dare move lest she draw back. Every cell feels like bursting.

Touch me, you bitch.

Four fingers, five, on and on she thrusts. I watch mesmerized as her hand becomes a fist and lunges incandescent through the night air. My body contracts again and again as her physical absence violates my aching need.

I can't stand it, I can't stand it.

Release comes. Wave after glorious wave of white-hot pleasure roars through my swollen nerves. Her hands deftly manifest each sweet surge as she signs her ecstasy and my own, time and time again.

I am aware of the sound of drums. They seem far away. I want them to stop. I crave silence. Deep, satisfying silence and the presence of Her. Thumping, pounding, dissonant drumming. Leave me be, I whisper. I want to stay here, with her, whose scent still lingers in the heavy air. My attention wavers and strays. Cautiously I open my eyes.

Boots and feet. Not drums. The wail of the disco floods into my brain. I'm at carnival and she's gone. Twenty thousand people and I feel alone. I sit up. My body is covered in fine red dust. Several bright feathers fall forward. They are attached to my hair, which is bound throughout with a string of tiny bells.

Of course making ourselves out to be nice girls isn't our only impulse as lesbians. For some of us, being as raw, raunchy, and unredeemable as possible becomes a political and sexual identity. More on that later.

Entirely concerned with sex

LIZARD: Our society's hatred for sex is profound. Not just gay sex, any sex. Lust by itself is suspect, obscene, perverse, dirty. I remember sitting at a lesbian dinner party talking about the sexual imagery that had just appeared in *Angles*. Why had the woman made those pictures? everyone kept asking. It was to represent lesbian love. No, it was to create feminist imagery. No, it was to shock straight people. Maybe she made them as a turn-on, I ventured. Silence. "You learned that from your father," someone finally said. The ultimate dismissal.

But I didn't learn that from my father!

What's so bad about sex for its own sake? No one seems to think they should only eat if they're in love.

But sex has to be redeemed by something. When it's done with the appropriately redeeming love, politics, or artistic merit, then sex becomes beautiful and important again, things it apparently can't be on its own.

"I wish you had used women who were really in love," writes one woman on the walls of DRAWING THE LINE. "I can deal with the s/m stuff here because of the obvious love between the women," writes another. "I feel ripped off—why didn't you show real lovers—this is fake sex, fake tenderness, fake love." "A beautiful portrait of two people in love—whether they're homo or hetero doesn't matter," writes a man. "Sex without love equals abuse," writes a woman.

What kind of love?, I wanted to ask her. I love Persimmon, but she's not my lover. Are these all photos of abuse, then? What about the sex you have with someone you should have broken up with months ago? Is it only real sex if it's good? Is it only real sex if you come, if you touch her cunt? If you say I love you? If no one's watching? If it's a spontaneous expression of love?

PERSIMMON: For many people, the issue of "real love" in lesbian sexual imagery is central. If the women are "really in love," photos will be hotter, better, truer. This assumption was tested in DRAWING THE LINE, which many people (who hadn't read our artists' statement) found to be a convincing portrait of True Lesbian Love. Others (who had read our artists' statement) found it inauthentic because of Lizard's and my non-traditional relationship. Most people assumed that the meaning they saw was inherent in the photos themselves, rather than their own creative contribution as audience.

How do you photograph love? What does it look like? We played with this question in TRUE INVERSIONS. Susan appears in the video section with her (real) lover, Ali. Is their sex hotter than Lizard's and mine? Is it more real?

At this point, I've done sex photos with two women who are my lovers as well as two women who aren't my lovers. My experience has been that being "real lovers" isn't the biggest difference. On camera, doing it with Lizard was very similar to doing it with my lovers.

Doing it for the camera is very different from doing it for yourselves. You might be turned on, but your turn-on isn't the point. The photo shoot is the point.

The camera isn't very accurate at recording emotion. This was brought home to me at a shoot that Susan and I did as part of an erotic photography workshop. The shoot was comfortable and fun, but when we got the contact sheets back, the photos were really heavy and frightening. Some of the workshop participants insisted that I must have been scared, there had to have been a "real" emotion that was caught in the look of terror on my face. But in fact, I was very relaxed and focussed on the the shoot as a vehicle for teaching. The terror was a construction of gesture and camera angle.

Shoots are like that. Sometimes at the moment of most intense openness and passion, what the camera catches is a weird shadow under your nose. You can shoot a whole roll of hot sex for that one shot that seems real and true to

VANCOUVER

You can't be a travelling lesbian sex goddess forever. Sooner or later you have to go back to where you're no big deal. Back to Vancouver, back to working part-time as a waitress, back to your ex-girlfriend who isn't speaking to you. Back to schmoozing at art openings as an alternative to staying home alone, wondering what you're doing with your life.

I've never been to an opening at the Van Herck Gallery before. They're well-catered invitation-only events, too rich for my blood. But tonight is different. Tonight is the group show called Brown Eyes, and I'm here with my very own invite. Hand delivered to me by Sushilla, because the artists' invitation lists were accidentally misplaced until it was too late to mail them out. The show had been full of accidents like that—paintings accidentally

Who

do I think you

are?

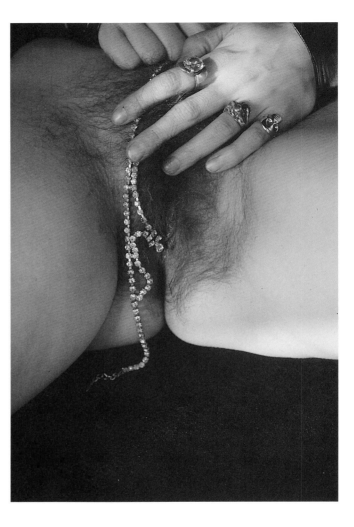

left in the storage room instead of hung, artists' statements accidentally edited, and Sharon Van Herck always sorry, but what could she do?

"She's the kind of white woman who thinks one multi-culti group show a year is affirmative action," Sushilla says, glaring across the room at the gallery owner. "It's like she's throwing us a bone to keep us quiet. And then she freaks out trying to control everything we do, and always with a sweet, sweet smile. Bitch. She gives lesbians a bad name."

"Yeah, last year she did the same thing, and

when someone complained she said they were censoring her. Creep." I glare too.

If looks could kill, Ms. Van Herck would be bleeding all over the tasteful taupe carpet, but she's deep in conversation with a woman in a red dress, oblivious to her shredded reputation. Red Dress is seriously cute and deserves better.

Meanwhile there's a pair of art students prowling the gallery. Scruffy butches, trying to look tough. They see Sushilla and me skulking behind a pillar, and converge on us. Sushilla perks up as one of

someone. And it's not because that one shot was taken at the one moment when you were really in love.

Visibility and transgression

SUSAN: Images of lesbians created by lesbians are extremely rare and difficult to find, yet photographs taken by men, of women staged to look like lesbians, are common fare in both porno mags and videos. Lesbians aren't fooled by these images. We know who they are meant for and sometimes they disgust and sadden us and sometimes we get turned on by them. When there is prolonged drought you tend to get less fussy about the purity of the water you drink.

It's all part of what some theorists call "reading across the grain." Some of us have been reading across the grain for so long that our eyes have splinters. We have taken what we could from heterosexual representations because there have been no other images to draw from.

When Kiss & Tell makes photographs or videos that include images of lesbian sex, we are venturing onto a hotly contested territory that feels hazardous, confusing, and utterly exhilarating. We give ourselves permission to represent whatever we want, to image *our own* sexuality, to show pictures of lesbians for lesbians. Imagine our surprise and the surprise of our viewers when our photographs sometimes look achingly familiar, so much so that some of them could be substituted directly into those nasty male porno mags. Worse yet, some of these images are hot. I wonder a lot about what that *hot* signifies.

I don't think it is just because we have seen porn before and have learned only one way to respond to images of lesbian sex. I think it has something to do with occupying forbidden territory, a retrieval of something we lost or perhaps never fully had, that we are finally claiming. That something is power. The act of taking a culturally degraded image of yourself and transforming it into something beautiful is a profoundly subversive act. One of the most satisfying aspects of producing lesbian sexual representations is the sweet freedom this transgression implies.

them compliments her work. The other is chatting me up, recognizes me from Kiss & Tell. Maybe I am a big deal after all, at least to student lesbians, at least when I stand around with a hot shot painter like Sushilla.

Over the student's shoulder, I can see the gallery owner talking intensely. Maybe the woman in the dress is a rich collector. She's still cute. She also looks a bit familiar. But it couldn't be.

I think these student butches planned all their moves. The one with beaded braids takes

Sushilla's arm and they drift off to look at the paintings. The crewcut one is standing very close as she talks to me. She's taller than I am; even in boots I have to look up. I'm not used to that, it's interesting. She looks straight into my eyes as she talks. That look, yes—I know that you know and what are you going to do about it? She wants to fuck me, and then she wants to tell all her friends at art school that she fucked me. That's interesting too.

It is now apparent that Ms. Van Herck is not

3. John Preston, "What Happened?" *Out/Look: National Lesbian and Gay Quarterly* 15 (Winter 1992): 8

LIZARD: As we affirm and celebrate our history (which we must), in my queer culture we celebrate a history of hidden clubs, closeted lives. We have an underground history, and we acknowledge it. We struggle to be visible, accepted, out. We support those who couldn't be, can't be. But the two desires—to be a strong underground culture, and to be a vibrant above-ground one, are in conflict.

John Preston, writing in *Out/Look,*[3] talks about this dilemma specifically in relation to the s/m community. Once an underground closed and secret society of ritual and mystery, it has become okay, defined, explored, accepted—at least in some parts of our community. And it has lost its charge for him. It was not long ago that many people in the gay and lesbian communities worked hard to unlearn what they had learned about s/m practitioners, and to destigmatize the practices. But without stigma, where is the transgression many people find essential to s/m?

I see this analysis as describing something parallel to many discussions about lesbianism and visibility. As a community, we have learned to feel good about what we have done with a very difficult situation. We are proud to be gay, and often proud not to be straight. We have even learned to see the advantages: our freedom to invent paradigms for ourselves; our anonymity; our ability to recognize each other on the street; our codes and signals and subversiveness.

But if being in the closet is stifling, so is being underground. We want our rights and we want to be seen. We fight for it, take risks because we love our culture so much. But when we are seen, it can mean that we give up some things from that same culture—our identity as invisible outcasts, for one thing.

Caucus versus ghetto. No one has resolved it.

SUSAN: An important element of lesbian images is the ways in which they build community. Lesbian photographs (published and unpublished) get circulated, passed hand to hand, discussed and debated in the community. There is a tremendous demand and need for self-representation by a community whose

closing a sale. She looks deep into the woman's eyes, that look, yes. She touches the woman's arm as they talk, her hand lingering a moment. I should have known rich collectors don't come to shows like this. The woman smiles at her, and then looks away, across the gallery. Our eyes meet for an electric second and then she's talking to Van Herck again.

Crewcut is looking that look, saying, "I've always found your work exciting."

"Oh yeah?" I say. "How exciting?"

She pushes me against the pillar. She holds me there, looking down at me for a minute, and then she presses her long body into mine. I can feel her soft little breasts through her T-shirt, but the rest of her is hard. Her hands are hard, pulling my shirt off one shoulder. Her kisses are hard. "Like that," she says, "exciting like that."

I almost can't resist her. But I have to know. I push her back a step, kiss her on the mouth.

"You're very sweet," I say. "You make my cunt wet."

psychic survival depends on the sure knowledge that there are others like ourselves.

Lesbian porn photos are important in that they provide entry into a lesbian context; however, these images will not necessarily be read as lesbian. How the photographs will be interpreted depends entirely on who is doing the viewing. Taken out of a specific lesbian context, lesbian porn can be easily referenced to straight porn and is often treated as such by male viewers. The format of some lesbian porn is very similar to straight "lesbian" porn. What is absent in both is a penis. But the heterosexual male spectator can effortlessly, and pleasurably, insert his own.

A provocative and radical aspect of lesbian photographic production is the alluring prospect of discovering new ways to portray lesbian desire and to locate the precise differences of this portrayal from heterosexual imagery. One way to contrast the two is to inscribe these differences across the entire spectrum of the production by not only taking responsibility for what is happening within the frame but also grappling with the various factors that contribute to its formation and development. These might include collective process, material considerations, community involvement, the site and context within which the representations are viewed, and the role of the spectator.

Interactions, collaborations, and feedback from various lesbian communities, on many different levels, can contribute to our productions. Lesbian artists have much to gain from building on each other's projects and efforts as we navigate the often treacherous terrain of self-representation both within and outside our specific communities. Ultimately, though, meaning occurs during viewer engagement and it is at that point that the producer relinquishes control. One of the most effective strategies a lesbian producer can have is to open up the door for a reading that is absolutely explicit in its message of *other than straight* in a bid to overturn heterosexist assumptions. This will not eliminate misinterpretation, but it will pave the way for strong and powerful representations which res-

onate with lesbian integrity and lesbian desire and which contribute to the self-definition of who we sense ourselves to be.

Inside the outside

LIZARD: The by-now familiar dictum, "We're here, we're queer, get used to it" is a neat way of solving the visibility/underground contradiction. Take on being invisible as your visible identity. In our desire to define ourselves politically and to include our diversity, we chose the word "queer." Now I feel "queer" has lost its focus. It can designate a political position, but it has also become a word to designate marginalized people, in some cases anyone on the margins. Unified by being outcast, we end up celebrating the state of outcastedness in and of itself. Celebrating it, and at the same time demanding that it be accepted. But doesn't acceptance de-marginalize it, destroy it? And then we are left with the search for a new margin.

I find my marginalization a poor basis for a politic. It feels like my community ends up constantly letting itself be defined by the power centre it is working against. I am more interested in looking for community definitions within our communities. But what would those definitions be?

And isn't transgression a turn-on? Yes. Maybe not a good basis for a politic, but perhaps an okay basis for sex.

The cult of the bad girl is well entrenched in lesbian culture. A button reading "Good girls go to heaven, bad girls go everywhere" was one of the very first gifts I got from my first lesbian lover. We're bad, the women your mother warned you about, outlaws in black leather jackets, rebels and misfits.

By now, how essential is that badness to my sexuality? How much of the lust that brought me here is lust for the margins, the invent-it-yourself periphery? It is my theory that lust and sex are a basic building block of lesbian and gay culture. Just lusting after someone of the same sex is a risk, and I live in a community of queer people who have taken this risk in order to follow their desires.

Then I walk back through the crowd.

I have to know.

I start to approach them and then lose my nerve. I've never met Sharon Van Herck. She doesn't deal with lowlife types like me. What's my opening line? Do I just walk up to them and say, "Excuse me, but I think I've fucked your friend?" I can't quite do it.

I walk around the gallery a bit, throwing glances at Ms. Red Dress. She looks at me too, and she has the right grey eyes. She has the stance with the legs. She has nice hands. I can't use my cunt as a barometer in the usual way, because of the persistent presence of the student butch. I am turned on, but I don't know which one is doing it to me. Maybe I should just go home, or wherever, with Crewcut. She obviously thinks my abrupt leave-taking was a come-on. She, too, is walking around the gallery, only she is trying to catch *my* eye. She has a forceful stride, and an almost teen awkwardness. I am thinking about her hard kisses. I am remembering her pushing me. She is moving closer to me in the crowd, and I don't know if I will resist

How important have risks become to *my* desires? How much of my sexuality is tied to how transgressive it is to do it?

SUSAN: At a time when lesbian images are beginning to be noticed and *read* as lesbian by the general public, a new and perhaps not unexpected development has emerged: mainstream appropriation. This appropriation diffuses and attempts to consume the radical possibilities that the *outside/outlaw* status of lesbianism signifies, and the very real threat that it poses to the stability of the dominant order which is based on compulsory heterosexuality. Some lesbians optimistically see this type of appropriation as a signal that lesbianism is becoming accepted and tolerated by the community at large. This would be a fitting response if a similar tolerance were reflected in the political, legal, and social conditions that constitute daily life, but unfortunately this isn't the case. Reaction to increased visibility of homosexuality has been swift and vicious, as increased incidents of gay-bashing and recently passed anti-gay legislation in the USA and England prove.

How are we to understand and interpret the contemporary queer dilemma of assimilation and appropriation? What does it mean that our images are reflected back to us through ad campaigns and TV talk shows—those flagships of social readiness, eagerly venturing forth onto the edge. The edge of the known world, the mysterious other—in this case queer-ness itself, that which is *not* heterosexual. How do we make sense of media lesbianism and its gloss of acceptability when at the same time our images and books are being confiscated and destroyed, ostensibly to protect the moral purity of the same masses who are tuned in to the *Geraldo* show?

One surprising thing is that the forbidden images, indefinitely detained behind the closed gates of Canada Customs, in police vaults, or on the desk of legislators, have a peculiar habit of re-surfacing in unlikely places. Not the exact images but inexact replicas. They turn up between the covers of haute-couture

this time. Why bother? Red Dress is obviously engaged with Van Bitch and couldn't care less.

I try not to look at either one.

It's very complicated.

Finally Red Dress is alone. She is walking over to the coffee urn. I intercept as casually as my cunt will let me.

"Hi. You look really familiar. Have we met?"

"I'll say," she says and laughs and laughs. "But I'd love to get to know you better."

It's Her. Halifax. She's so fucking insolent. I can't think of a single snappy comeback.

"Do you want a drink?" she asks.

"No," I say.

"Don't sulk," she says in her best sultry voice, and sashays off to the bar. I stand rooted, waiting for her return. She picks up two drinks (insolent!) and is on her way back when Van Herck cuts in smoothly, ready to take up where she left off. Damn. I start across the gallery, determined to interrupt them this time, no matter how awkwardly.

Crewcut comes up behind me. She lets her hand

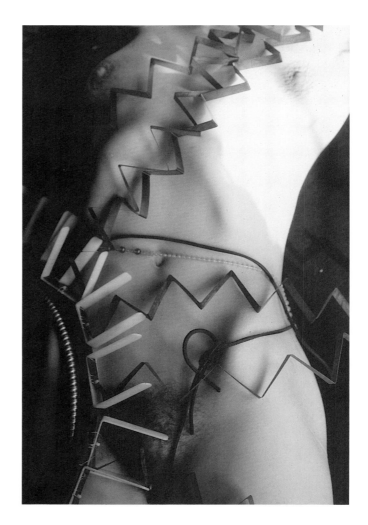

Do I look

like a lesbian?

graze my ass as she moves around me, and I move in response, without thinking.

"Are you running away from me?" Crewcut asks.

"I'm not sure," I say.

Crewcut takes that as encouragement, and drapes her arm around my waist. Halifax chooses that moment to desert Van Herck and bring me my drink. Orange juice. She checks out Crewcut, and laughs. "Slut," she says to me under her breath.

I've got this wet cunt and I don't know which way to turn.

I'm struggling with how I am going to introduce them. I am sure that the fact that we fuck is written all over my face, but I still don't know her name, and I find this embarrassing. Come to think of it, I don't know Crewcut's name either. What should I say—"Ms. Almost Fuck, meet Ms. More Frequent Fuck?"

Needless worries. They know each other, of course. I can't figure out from their conversation how they know each other, but they're not going to be separated now, I can tell. They're talking about

magazines, or in best-selling photo books, or in mainstream films, or on bill-boards advertising men's underwear. Turned up and out in a material world and sold back to us—us queers—newly recognized for our market potential and our flair for the original.

Capitalism exploits consumer desire for that which is different, marginalized. When encountering advertising images of *the lesbian* or *the queer*, the consumer is being encouraged to embrace difference by assuming the look of difference, thus further diffusing the power of actual transgression by defusing the potency of its signs. Advertisers and other commercially motivated ventures such as Madonna's photography book *Sex*[4], blatantly appropriate lesbian cultural signs. In *Sex*, Madonna's "blonde ambition" drapes itself over the danger-ous transgressive sexuality of two radical leather dykes, titillating straight sensibilities with an indrawn breath, a momentary suspension of safety and its attendant adrenalin-rush value, at the same time underscoring the certainty that this experience is a mere throw-away exchange. One merely needs to turn the page to find our intrepid heroine safely back in the arms of men or inserting her body between the bodies of a heterosexual black couple in her quest to conquer ever new transgressive frontiers.

4. Madonna, *Sex* (New York: Warner Books, 1992).

LIZARD: I have a friend who mused to me that she wonders sometimes if she would be a lesbian if things were different. It puts her where she wants to be in relation to the mainstream. Her lust is mingled with her desire to situate herself outside the patriarchy. If in fact gender is not locked to nature, sexuality is not immutable, how much of what we lust after is just plain danger—for some of us the danger of living with a girlfriend in the suburbs (and that *is* dangerous)?

I saw a performance by Christine Taylor, a bisexual woman, in which she talked about her lust for gay men, and her distaste for straight ones. I am a lesbian, but I could relate. How can you lust after a straight man? But a man whose sexuality endangers him and you? Aaah.

some groovy film I never saw, some mutual friend I never met, some art school scandal I never heard about. In a few minutes I have gone from the deliciously agonizing dilemma of choosing between the two of them, to wondering if I shouldn't make myself scarce so they can be alone. If I made some cutting remark and stormed off, would they come after me? The only reason I don't is because of Crewcut's electrifying and possessive hold on my hip.

I look away and catch sight of Van Herck, glaring

at them. I can almost sympathize, but not quite.

They start making plans—lunch, coffee, the art school grad show. My mind wanders. Why doesn't Halifax look at me? Why didn't I take the hard kisses when I had the chance?

"That's okay, isn't it?" Crewcut is asking me a question.

"What?" I say.

"It's okay if we stop on the way, isn't it? She has to pick up a couple of things."

On the way where? I wonder, though I must

The search for sexual danger? Sometimes I think that is where a lot of my fantasies come from. Not from an inherent lesbianness, but from that queerness, renegadeness, danger. Fantasizing lesbian sex, sex in public, sex with strangers, they don't work any more. Aaah, but sex with a man, that would be transgressive. So I fantasize about the lesbian parties where I bring my boyfriend.

And then I find out that lesbians are doing that, having boyfriends. I am not surprised. Someone is always out there acting out my fantasy. I don't want to dismiss someone's sexuality lightly, but I do sometimes think the motivation behind newer better badder practices is just the search for ever more transgression. It's an endless and self-perpetuating progression, constantly in reaction to itself, swinging from transgression to acceptance to new transgression. Nothing deflates a sex radical as quickly as indifference.

Even as I write this I am uncomfortable with what I am saying. I don't want to imply that anyone finds it a turn-on to be trashed in the way sexual outlaws have been. When s/m dykes were expelled from conferences in the early eighties, none of them said they enjoyed it. But I do think that those conflicts have now become part of the identity of the sexual outsider.

I was at a panel at International Lesbian Week in Vancouver in 1991, where a woman in black leather stood up and complained about how she used to know what black leather meant and she doesn't anymore. At one time, wearing black leather in a feminist situation was a signal that required great courage to display. It is almost meaningless now. It doesn't mean secret s/m society anymore. Now it means "I have money." Is this because of appropriation? Changing fashions? A whole community lusting for transgression until we kill it?

Can we have it both ways?

THE ABHORRENT LESBIAN SHOW

I most definitely do not endorse this. It's totally inappropriate.

—KEN KOWALSKI, Deputy Premier of Alberta[1]

. . . the straight mind develops a totalizing interpretation of history, social reality, culture, language, and all the subjective phenomena at the same time . . . The consequence of this tendency toward universality is that the straight mind cannot conceive of a culture, a society where heterosexuality would not order not only all human relationships but also its very production of concepts . . .

—MONIQUE WITTIG[2]

LIZARD: I still use the word "queer," despite feeling it has been diluted, flattened. I think of it still as a sharp word, designate it still to mean sexual difference, sexual courage, sexual enigma. And I make art for queers first, cherish queer praise, wince at queer criticism. I want straights and the art world to be there, but do I care what they think? If they don't laugh, does that mean there is no joke? They live with me, down the hall, share an office, but they don't live here, in my queer city.

1. "Tax-Funded Gay Sex Play 'God-awful'," *Edmonton Sun*, 15 Jan. 1993, p. 24.

2. Monique Wittig, "The Straight Mind," in her *The Straight Mind and Other Essays* (Boston, Beacon Press, 1992), 27-28.

My city is crafted by lust and love. It is not always beautiful, there are huge gulfs of inequality and silence, but I cannot escape it. I come to it and from it.

The performance art that we do in Kiss & Tell builds directly on a tradition in Vancouver of lesbian sex shows. Our work is a hybrid of experiences of lesbian sexuality, built by three lesbians of different classes, abilities, histories, futures. It borrows from contemporary art and traditional European theatre, and is blessed, I think, by a lack of formal training. It owes its biggest debt to debates and conversations among lesbians and feminists. Our biggest errors have come when we forget this debt, try to speak for, instead of with.

At our shows, if the audience is mostly lesbian, somehow we already know each other, even if they've never heard of us before. Sometimes they are laughing before the show starts, charged and ready. Up there I can feel them with me, feel the apprehension about the sex, feel the power as we and they together move with the text and the images—the headiest experience I could hope to have.

It doesn't take much, slightly smaller numbers, a slightly different percentage of queers, to change this entirely. The not-queers are not even necessarily homophobic, just polite, just lost, just don't know whether they should laugh, can laugh. And the lesbians are silent too, kept in their place. Reaching to them from the stage then is an act of faith, not a shared experience but an individual one. What is the critical mass that makes the shift? How many queers to make it ours?

For those hets who hate us, one queer is too many. Five queers together means we're taking over the world. Special rights. Reverse discrimination. Politically correct censorship. These phrases are weapons they fire at the smallest challenge to their right to control everything, to name the world in their own image. This is the backlash all oppressed people know.

It seems boring to have to say it again, but white straight men rule the art world. Rule the Western world, actually. There is still a tendency to see art by anyone else as an aberration, particular, "other." I don't have trouble with the idea that queer art has meanings that only queers really understand. I do have

admit I am heartened by Crewcut's assumption that we will all leave together. Maybe we will still talk about my art and how exciting it is. Crewcut helps Her on with her coat, very smooth. Halifax grabs my collar and brings her head close. "Slut," she says again. Crewcut doesn't seem to notice, or if she does, she approves. Across the gallery, Sharon Van Herck watches us leave.

What have I agreed to?

Our stop is at a two-story penthouse twenty floors above the beach. Halifax has many keys—to the parkade, to the elevator, to the security system. I feel like a burglar.

"What is this joint?" I ask as Halifax unlocks the three bolts on the apartment door.

"Haven't you been here before?" she asks with dangerous innocence. "It's Sharon Van Herck's place."

I have never seen an apartment anything like this. It is filled with art and expensive furniture. Crewcut is wandering around the immense living

trouble with the idea that straight art is universal and my art isn't. That the queer audience doesn't count.

In November 1992, Kiss & Tell performed our piece TRUE INVERSIONS at the Banff Centre for the Arts. The audience was composed mostly of straight artists. There were also lesbians in the audience, some of them artists, some from Calgary and Banff.

Even though we sorely missed the strong lesbian presence, one straight reviewer in the audience saw many lesbians there. Rick Bell, writing for the *Alberta Report*,[3] talks about an audience full of cheering crewcut lesbians. Where were they all? we joked as we read his review. Later it wasn't funny any more, when that review (which contained many more serious inaccuracies than the number of lesbians he saw) ended up on the desk of the Deputy Premier of Alberta. He called a press conference where he referred to TRUE INVERSIONS as "this abhorrent lesbian show" (see note 1) and asked his fellow cabinet ministers to help put an end to homosexual shows at government-funded institutions. It wasn't at all funny when we became the subject of discussion in the Alberta Legislature. When our show became the justification for attacking the Banff Centre's funding. When the review was used as the basis to threaten arm's-length funding for Alberta arts groups.

In the months that followed, lesbians, gays, and arts groups across Alberta demonstrated against censorship. There were articles, editorials, debates, and radio shows.

And except for the 150 or so people who had actually seen our show, they were all basing their positions on the review in the *Alberta Report*, even the people who supported us.

People who had never seen the show looked no further than Rick Bell's article for the facts. He said there was a video of us masturbating, so our right to masturbate on video was attacked and defended. That's fine, but in the 30-minute video, there are about 7 minutes of talking about masturbation and

3. Rick Bell, "Kissing and Telling in Balmy Banff," *Alberta Report,* 7 December 1993, p. 33.

room saying Wow, and Cool, every few seconds. But I refuse to be impressed. I follow Halifax to the foot of a curving staircase. I can't even pretend to be calm.

"What are we doing here? Are you a friend of Sharon Van Herck's? Do you know what that bitch did to my friend? Why do you have her keys?" Are you fucking her? is what I really want to ask. How could you, with someone like that?

Halifax pauses on the first step. "How did I get her keys? I know her cleaning lady. We're tres-

passing." She turns and runs lightly up the stairs before I can get my mouth closed. My heart makes a swift transition from abject jealousy to abject fear. Why does She do these things to me?

Crewcut is making herself at home, building a fire in the marble fireplace with the cupid-strewn mantelpiece over it.

"You'd better not do that. We're not supposed to be here. We'd better just wait by the door and be ready to split."

"Relax," she says.

about 3 seconds of actual hands on genitals. Three seconds in a 30-minute video. The power of the press! The power of that one straight man!

And underlying everything was the assumption that we had nothing to say. We're just a bunch of dykes, to be tolerated, if you're on "our" side, but without analysis or opinions about what was going down. Just like journalists don't phone hookers to find out what they think about anti-prostitution laws, they don't ask queers how we feel about anti-gay arts laws. We're all expected to be grateful for the visibility, for the reporters who think it's okay that we show a masturbation video when we don't! I am not grateful. I want you to get it right. Crumbs are not enough.

SUSAN: I believe most of us who have grown up in North America learn to censor ourselves, and others, from a very early age. We learn to distinguish good pictures from dirty pictures, good stories from bad stories. We know which magazines get hidden under the mattress and where the naughty books are shelved in the library. We know when to say "yuck" and "gross" at the appropriate moments when watching TV or at the movies with our friends. The amazing thing is that we can learn these things by some kind of cultural osmosis. We don't need to be told. Most of us are indoctrinated with the same values.

I grew up in a small town where nobody talked about sex but it was on everybody's mind. I knew this because I was a popular baby-sitter about town. When the little tykes were safely tucked away in bed I would begin my sleuthing. Not for me the TV reruns, or the homework sitting on the kitchen counter. I was a girl with a mission, a fact-finding mission. I wanted to find out everything I could about what nobody would talk about: sex. In the minister's house I found the marital aid, a small white book given to brides to prepare them for *the* night they would be losing *it*. In the butcher's house I found adult comics under the bed. In my friend's sister's trailer I found *True Romance*. This was sex education, home-schooling style.

The only other way to find stuff out was by listening to adults talk to each other. That's where I heard about the local mother who was turning her only child into a sissy. "Why, did you see how she had him dressed at Sunday school, all prissy-like? Mark my words, no good will come of it." Or, "You won't understand this, but I don't want you to play with X anymore. Mrs. W. saw her doing *a bad thing* with a boy through the bedroom window." Or, "There's something weird about those children, rotten home life, but it's none of our business, you just stay away from those kids."

So I learned that sex was secret, dirty, and bad, and that images and stories about sex were worse. I began to censor myself. I bought *True Romance* comics and I hid them. I became friends with the prissy boy and we traded drawings we'd done of women with lots of curves (wearing tight, imaginative evening gowns), and we threw them off the bridge. A few years later, on a continuation of a theme, I would tell my parents I was off to the high school basketball game and end up in the bowling alley parking lot learning how to French kiss. Like the adults in my town, I was learning how to lead a double life and become adept at the fine art of deception and censorship.

It took years to unravel this knot and find ways of coming to my own truths about sex. I still mistrust my judgement at times. When I want to censor some part of Kiss & Tell's work, for example, where is this impulse coming from? Is it really the ubiquitous State I am so concerned about, or is it the nosey neighbour of my past peering through the bedroom window?

Reverend sir. Take your eyes off me, asshole. You know I don't want to be here, don't you, creep. You know my parents make me come here. Let go of my hand you sweaty God-fuck, dead shit. Pouring your syrupy words over us like thick molasses. Making all those stupid promises about the promised land. How come your kids are always dressed in those cutesy little outfits? A different one every Sunday and you telling my daddy to give money. I hate this scratchy stupid dress, same one every week,

"No, we could really get in trouble. Van Herck could walk in and call the cops."

"Come on, she's still at the opening. She'll be there for hours. And anyway, if we hear her coming, we can leave by the fire escape."

"Oh sure, and climb down 20 stories. That'll be fun."

Crewcut is grinning from ear to ear. I hover near the door for another minute and then give it up. I'm not prepared to walk away, so I might as well accept the situation. Maybe Halifax has it all in hand, like that night on the Edmonton rooftop. She hasn't gotten me killed. Yet.

"Just how well do you know my friend?" I ask Crewcut.

She shrugs, still grinning, and reaches for my hand.

Not so fast, I think, as I perch on the edge of a straight-backed chair. Crewcut sprawls across the thick fur rug in front of the fireplace. Some endangered species, no doubt. The firelight on her strong body, the soft fur, it's like every clichéd sex

pinching me at the neck, too tight everywhere, itching my legs with that stiff lace stuff, a dog wouldn't sleep on it.

—SUSAN (from TRUE INVERSIONS)

PERSIMMON: When I first heard of Andres Serrano's "Piss Christ," it was being denounced from the U.S. Senate floor as an obscene sacrilege. I heard about it on the TV news and read editorials both pro and con. There was never a picture of it, but the descriptions didn't fill me with a great desire to see it. I knew what it was about: a photograph of a crucifix submerged in a gallon of the artist's urine. It sounded to me like one of those boring avant-garde one-liners of the let's-think-of-something-shocking-to-prove-how-daring-we-are school. Irritating, but still in need of defense from right-wing censors.

Two years later, I finally saw the photograph—one of the most beautiful, disturbing, and (there's no other word for it) spiritual images I've ever seen. Both the piss and what appeared to be a cheap plastic crucifix were made radiant and mysterious, filled with deep golden light. This was no gimmick art, but a subtly constructed and deeply moving meditation on the nature of holiness and profanity (with holiness winning, hands down).

Or at least that's what I saw.

The *Alberta Report* review of TRUE INVERSIONS is incredibly accurate in some ways. The quotes are practically word for word. Rick Bell probably had a tape recorder. And yet he gets almost everything wrong. What he saw was filtered through his own experiences, politics, and expectations. Reading his review, you could easily imagine what the show was like: one of those boring self-consciously avant-garde performance art things of the me-and-my-friends-are-so-artsy-cool-and-daring school. Irritating, but still in need of defense from right-wing censors.

Having the right-wing interpretation of a work become the Official Story

story I ever read. But I must admit, it gets to me. Fuck this. I want to know what Halifax is doing before I commit to anything.

I barely have time to finish the thought before she comes into the room and throws something into Crewcut's lap. Condoms. And she called *me* a slut . . .

She slides down next to Crewcut, who pulls her close and starts playing with the strap of her dress. They both look at me.

I get the distinct impression it's my move.

But I can't move an inch. I'm mesmerized by the sight of Crewcut's hand playing with that strap. The way her fingers slide across Her skin and get tangled in the thin band of silk, the way the strap slips off Her shoulder exposing the top of her breast. I realize I've been staring and I raise my eyes to Halifax's. They are wicked in the flickering light.

Still watching me she puts her hand behind Crewcut's head and guides it to her breast. Crewcut slips both straps over Halifax's shoulders and eases the dress down to her waist. I recognize

Spot the

invisible

disablility.

the soft skin that Crewcut tenderly strokes, the erect nipples that she flicks with her tongue and slips sweetly between her lips. I feel my own nipples responding as I remember the taste.

Crewcut is sliding her hands under Her red dress. They start to kiss and Halifax is kneading Crewcut's ass.

I want to be Crewcut. I want to be Halifax.

I hear myself moan.

Halifax looks up and gazes directly into my eyes.

What a fucking bitch. I could feign being indifferent but we both know that I'm not. Watching these two touch is making me burn. It should be me. My mouth, my breast, Her touch, my skin. Damn Her. Damn both of them. I hate them. I'm angry, jealous, and thoroughly aroused.

Still looking at me, Halifax wraps her legs around Crewcut, whose face is buried in red silk. She blows me a kiss over Crewcut's shoulder and winks.

That does it. I stand up to leave, hesitate, and sit down again. I realize I don't want to leave. I *want* to watch. And she knows it.

seems to be a fairly common experience. Why does that happen? How does it work? What does it mean?

TRUE INVERSIONS comes out of specific communities, at a specific point in time. We are addressing issues and debates that are ongoing within our communities—issues like censorship and allegations of censorship; how past sexual abuse affects our present sexuality; the way that "whiteness" is seen as normal and universal; s/m; butch/femme; the constructed nature of sexual imagery; and the effect that a lesbian identity has on our relationships with our mothers.

Oh fuck, it's a hymn again. Oh mama, your voice embarrasses me the way it doesn't sound so good. I just pretend to sing, move my mouth a little but nothing comes out. It's all too loud already, deafeningly loud. Shut up, people. Stop singing. There ain't nothing to sing about. It's all a pack of lies. Can't you see what a liar sir is? He's the devil, he's the one. Not those poor sinners he's so bent on saving.

—SUSAN (from TRUE INVERSIONS)

Many of these issues are contentious within our communities, but the context of our disagreements is pretty clear—we've been having these arguments for a while. You can say "the Sex Debates," and lots of people will know which debates about whose sex.

We didn't make TRUE INVERSIONS to explain The Lesbian Lifestyle to straight people in hopes that they would see that we're actually okay, and decide to be nice to us. If that was what we had wanted to do, we would have made a very different piece of work. And we certainly didn't write it with right-wing homophobes in mind as our major audience. So it's no wonder Rick Bell was confused.

He says: "With photos of nude women projected on a screen behind them, the performers shared their fantasies and experiences of sex with other women."

The phrase "photos of nude women" conjures up pictures of lots of anonymous women. But *we* were the "nude women" in the slides. They are portraits

They are on the floor. Halifax is on her hands and knees facing me. Crewcut is behind her. Whatever Crewcut is doing with her hands, Halifax loves it. Panting and moaning deeply, she gasps, "Enjoying yourself, voyeur?" She is not so cool now. Her need is naked in her eyes.

"Come here," she demands, "kiss me."

I don't move. I can't. Crewcut turns her over and kisses her passionately.

She meant *me*. My tongue, her tongue, my lips, her teeth.

Crewcut is maneuvering Halifax back on her knees so her ass rests against Crewcut's crotch. Halifax looks up at me and her hot eyes are laughing. "Fuck me," she murmurs.

Fuck you.

I look at Crewcut. I remember the way her hard body felt as it pressed against mine at the gallery. I can feel my wet cunt contracting.

Crewcut is undoing her jeans with one hand as she fondles her companion's breasts. Halifax tears open a condom and smoothly passes it to Crewcut.

and self-portraits, photographed by Susan and conceptualized by all three of us. They are dream-like images of our own naked bodies. We have the power of the microphones, simultaneously with the vulnerability of nakedness. But the reviewer didn't notice (or didn't understand it to be of any consequence) that they were representations of ourselves.

I think part of what he missed are the particular kinds of relationships that women in general, and lesbians in particular, have to sexual imagery. On the covers of women's magazines in every supermarket check-out line, we see extremely provocative and sexualized pictures of half-clothed women. These images are presented to women not as "objects of desire" but as images for us to identify with and aspire to. In North American culture, these images shape most (lesbian as well as straight) women's ways of seeing sexualized pictures of other women, as well as our relationships to our own bodies. When I put my plump, 40-year-old body in front of the camera, this is the context I am addressing; a very different context from that of straight male consumers of commercial porn.

For lesbians, our relationship to images is more confusing still. Photographs of "nude women" could represent yourself, or they could represent a woman you desire. For lesbians (and bisexuals and gay men) the line between subject and object in a sexual image is much more slippery than for heterosexuals. This is further complicated by other aspects of our identities. If the photo was of, say, a lesbian in a wheelchair, would an able-bodied lesbian viewer have the same slippage between subject and object, or would she automatically distance herself, and see the woman in the photo as "other"? Gay Asian video artist Richard Fung addresses this issue in relation to race:

> Although I agree with Waugh that in gay as opposed to straight porn "the spectator's position in relation to the representations are open and in flux"[5] this observation applies only when all the participants are white. Race introduces another dimension that may serve to close

5. Tom Waugh, "Men's Pornography: Gay vs. Straight," *Jump Cut* 30 (March 1985): 31. Cited in Richard Fung, "Looking for My Penis" (see note 6).

Underneath the jeans I can see black leather straps encircling her body.

"Fuck me," Halifax says again.

No, fuck me. Fuck me senseless.

Crewcut is pressing against Her. I imagine the hard dildo pushing into her cunt. All I can see is a cloud of red silk and Crewcut's hands driving it forward and back against her own hips. I pretend they are my hands and that I can feel the body I know so well as I drive it onto my own hard cock over and over.

First I am being fucked, then I'm doing the fucking, savouring each possibility, each raw moment. Pure hunger. I want both of them. Now.

Halifax is looking at me again, sweet desire in her eyes. I start to smile as I realize how I will get her back for this.

I get off my chair and reach for Crewcut.

And then I hear the sound of a key in the lock.

down some of this mobility. This is not to suggest that the experience of gay men of color with this kind of sexual representation is the same as that of heterosexual women with regard to the gendered gaze of straight porn... A shifting identification may occur despite racially defined roles, and most gay Asian men in North America are used to obtaining pleasure from all-white pornography. This, of course, goes hand in hand with many problems of self-image and self-identity.[6]

6. Richard Fung, "Looking for My Penis," in *How Do I Look,* ed. Bad Object Choices (Seattle: Bay Press, 1991), 153-54.

We have many complex, conflicted relationships to sex pictures. Rick Bell erased these realities, projecting what is a particular straight, white male viewpoint onto the images, the audience, and the performers.

Remember how you would bore into me with your eyes as you clutched my sweaty hand? Did you see my hatred and resistance or were you more inclined to noticing the white smooth curve of my cheek and the shiny braids and the pink bows?

Hey, the church is nothing compared to your coup de grâce, your ultimate re-deeming tactic, hey reverend daddy? That neat laying-on-of-hands trick of yours in the hospital room. How you'd just have yourself a little out-loud conversation with your all-mighty father above about this girl's soul wanting and needing to stay put in that little girl body. Stupid fuck-head. Maybe I wanted that one-way ticket to ride. One thing for sure, I want you and your pals to get your stinking hands off my body right now.

—SUSAN (from TRUE INVERSIONS)

A similar point occurs in his version of the story that Lizard performs. He states that she is lusting after "any woman in a white lab coat." What Lizard actually says is: "I realize I'm aware of one other woman at work. She's tall. She wears

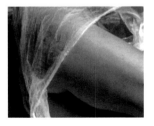

glasses. She's a very hard worker. She wears a white lab coat, and I can't tell what she's wearing underneath. She takes notes." He turns the story of a wild crush on a specific co-worker into a generalized erotic fetish for women in white lab coats. Why? The thing about this one particular woman that Lizard repeats over and over is *not* her white lab coat (which is never mentioned again), but the fact that she's a very hard worker.

When we were talking with our (heterosexual) acting coach, Penelope Stella, about this strange review, she said, "He just didn't understand Lizard's story. Eroticizing a woman for being hard-working and competent is a very lesbian thing."

But why does Rick Bell focus so much on Lizard's story, without even mentioning the story I read, which was the more obvious one to attack? Lizard's story concerns a shy and dorky woman who becomes overwhelmed by lust for a co-worker. At points in the performance when Susan and I are deep in the throes of sex, Lizard is still trying to figure out how to talk to the woman she's interested in. When we have performed for largely lesbian audiences, Lizard's character is the one who gets the most laughs—the one, I suspect, that most lesbians identify with.

My character is an artist, struggling with the power politics of an art opening. "Everyone's trying to impress everyone else and no one's listening," she says. "I'm doing it too, and I hate myself for it." Feeling outclassed by an art critic who is flirting with her girlfriend, she goes into the alley with her girlfriend, pushes her around, slaps her, and has sex with her.

This scene involves consensual s/m between two people who have apparently been doing this kind of thing together for a long time. It's placed in the context of the painful economic power relations that rule other areas of their lives.

When we have performed for largely lesbian audiences, there is a point, when my character slaps her girlfriend, when we can feel a large part of the audience

TORONTO

"As I recall," I heard a voice on the other side of the bookshelves say, "as I recall, you promised to do anything I wanted."

Hearing that one sentence sent me right back to the last time I had seen Halifax—two months ago, in a different town. Lying in her bed, her hand in my cunt, my head swimming, the universe unfolding, I *had* promised to do anything for her. Twenty minutes later, dreamy and listless, she had asked me to write the rest of her paper that was due the next day.

"As I recall," she had said in response to my indignation, "as I recall, you promised to do anything I wanted."

"It's a figure of speech," I said. "Just something I say for sex."

"For sex."

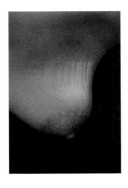

tense up. It feels like they're deciding whether to walk out or wait and see. Only a few people have ever actually walked out, but it's an intense moment. In the lesbian community, s/m is an area of great conflict, and when we bring it up in our show, the anger and confusion of those debates are right there in the audience.

We have performed three times for audiences that were predominantly heterosexual: once at the Vancouver East Cultural Centre, and twice at Banff. One of the differences is that, in all three of those performances, there was no moment of tension, of rejection, around slapping the girlfriend. This lack of reaction to the s/m content from straight audiences was not what we were expecting. If anything, we would have expected people who were less familiar with the debates within the lesbian community to find it *more* shocking. But this was definitely not the case.

One factor in their lack of response could be that, as sympathetic straight people, aware of how much judgement we already receive from the straight world, they didn't feel it was their place to pass judgement on any form of sexuality we presented. Another factor, more applicable to the *Alberta Report,* is that for many straight people, any lesbian sex is kinky at best, and the s/m stuff would be just one more perversion among perversions.

One of Rick Bell's most amazing interpretations was of a scene from our video where I pace the floor, fully clothed, in an angry interaction with the camera:

> I don't like to masturbate—I'm not going to do it for you now . . . I know my body, a million miles away, says it feels good, but it doesn't feel good . . . It's not fun, it just makes me feel weird. I feel nothing. Or it hurts . . . Did you never fuck when you didn't want to fuck? And you couldn't say I don't want to, and you couldn't say don't do this, and you couldn't say it hurts, and you couldn't even cry?

"Yes."
And that had seemed to be the end of it.

Now here I stood in the university bookstore, perusing anthologies with incomprehensible titles, preparing to give another guest lecture to a Women's Studies class, and suddenly I was sent right back. I felt that room, that hand. I would do anything for her, for that. I had to know if it was Her on the other side of those shelves.

Two laughing women emerged from the next aisle and were moving toward the cash register.

Did the taller one look at me as they went by?

I had come here to get something, what was it? Which book? I needed a book, but I had to decide fast, the two women were almost at the cash. The books were arranged by course, so I made a snap decision to buy all the books on the course list for the class I was talking to that afternoon.

Did she look at me? Were those Her eyes?

I looked in my wallet—$7.50. What's VISA for? I thought, and headed for the cash. Phew, the two

For anyone familiar with common after-effects of sexual abuse, the meaning of this monologue is clear: it talks about the way that past memories of sexual abuse can come up again, getting in the way of present sexual pleasure, bringing old feelings of pain and self-protective numbness. For some of us, sex is a minefield that we're sick of walking through, wondering what's going to blow up in our faces. Some of us give it up for a while—some give up forever.

But that wasn't what Rick Bell understood from that scene. He wrote: "The artists also showed a film featuring . . . a sexually repressed 'square' whining petulantly that sex with other women 'was not fun, it makes me feel weird'."

Who? Where? I guess he thinks we're these kinky free-love lesbian chicks, and anything that's not a fun fun party party attitude towards lesbian sex must be some straight thing we're making fun of. It reminds me of the characters played by women in a lot of straight porn videos. They're so strange. There's no *intensity* to them. They're all into no strings/no foreplay sex as often as possible with whoever's around. Are they what he's seeing when he sees us?

His image of lesbian sex artists doesn't seem to include us sometimes hating sex, and giving space and validation to that experience. He can't see what doesn't fit his image of us.

All this shit to get through to get to our pleasure. I'm trying hard to love this body. Back when I was younger the body would betray me. Exuberance would bare skin to soft breezes. Shame, shame, indecent girl. Act like a lady. What lady? I'd think. I don't see any ladies here. Just mothers. Beaten down, dowdy, grey, unhappy mothers. Mothers ready to betray their beautiful daughters for a few scant points from daddy. Please mama please, don't tell daddy. I promise I'll never do it again, I swear mama, oh don't tell him. I'll die if you tell him. I didn't mean to do it. Oh please mama, please mama, please mama . . .

—SUSAN (from TRUE INVERSIONS)

women were moving through the line slowly, something about cheque approval, and then too large a sub-total, a returned volume. The tall one brushed me on her way to stick the offending volume back on the shelf.

"That book is only $15 downtown," I heard her say to the cashier when she got back, "as I recall."

Our eyes locked.

Her?

I was stuck with $100 worth of books.

They moved out of the store. I casually followed,

armed with theory: Julia Kristeva, Judith Butler, Kaja Silverman, Birgit Odenso. Not for me the easily dismissed arguments of Andrea Dworkin and Susan Griffin. I had come a long way from there. I had been a visiting lecturer four times already. I had started by faking it, but by now I was the real thing. I was a tough customer, well troped and psychoanalyzed, hegemonic and meta-consumed.

They went to the library. Excellent. I know how to cruise libraries.

The right wing sees itself as under attack. In a view of the world that I can't recognize, they feel that "liberal" thought rules, that our society kowtows to the rule of political correctness, that gays and lesbians want to have more rights than heterosexuals, that whites are an oppressed minority suffering from reverse discrimination. This is the defensive anger of Aryan Nation, but it also wears more respectable clothes. A Reform Party candidate in the 1993 federal election in Canada was quoted as saying, "If you're a woman, coloured, and a lesbian, you're laughing all the way to the bank."[7] There's constant talk of the power of "special interest groups" (read female, disabled, queer, of colour), as compared to "ordinary Canadians" (read male, able bodied, het, white).

7. Colyne Gibbons, quoted in the *Vancouver Province*, 15 October 1993.

This is the context of right-wing readings of culture: from this defensive posture, Andres Serrano is seen as attacking Christianity, not (as he sees himself) examining the symbols of his own culture.

So who gets to say what "Piss Christ" means—me or Jesse Helms? Or Andres Serrano? Or you? Is there one version that's the true version, and are all others misinterpretations? Or are images meaningless except for the varying and equally valid interpretations we place on them? What does it mean to say all interpretations are equal in a Euro-American culture where inequality is institutionalized; where some versions are printed in every newspaper and other versions disappear?

8. *The Watson Witness* [Canora, Sask.], 6 January 1993.

9. *Hanna Herald* [Hanna, Alta.], 20 January 1993.

10. *West-Central Crossroads* [Kindersley, Sask.], 6 January 1993.

SUSAN: One offshoot of the *Alberta Report* article was a syndicated story that appeared in at least twenty little community papers sprinkled throughout Alberta, Manitoba, and environs. Written by Kevin Avram, the article was given titles like "Even Lesbianism is Government Funded,"[8] and "Government Coffers are Never Empty for 'Art',"[9] and "Tax Dollars Funding Smut."[10] To my mind, this article was more insidiously damaging than its predecessor, and more effective in furthering a deeply homophobic right-wing agenda. Having never seen

She sat down at a table in the reference room, her friend walked on to the carrels. I piled my books on the table, picked up Birgit Odenso, and began to read conspicuously. (It can be done. The important thing is to keep the title visible—(if it's a good one)—and alternate staring off into space, flipping back for reference, and making notes in the margins. Exclamation points look really good later. Steer clear of question marks.)

When I had established myself as a Thinker, I

hazarded a glance down the table. She was reading an Archie comic.

I returned to my books, somewhat less enthusiastically. She had a very familiar look, but could it be Halifax? I mean, by now I was used to her changing a lot, but she had always had an analysis. Now I was cruising some college student who thought the library was a good place to read comics.

I filled my margins with exclamation points! I lusted after this college student, whoever she

our show, Avram built on the distortions of the *Alberta Report* article. His article focussed discussion on the rights of the taxpayer whose dollars were being spent on a government-funded lesbian "ménage-à-trois." Of course there was no mention of the fact that lesbians pay taxes too.

But even as this type of hate-mongering and misinformation makes me angry, it isn't the first thing I think about when I consider those small-town papers and the people who are reading them. It is rural homosexuals and the young people who haven't fixed on their sexual identities that I wonder about, and the effect this type of homophobia has on them and their lives. When the only information you read about lesbian culture is through the lens of the Rick Bells and Kevin Avrams of this world, what does that do to your self-worth and fear of discovery?

It also makes me question what the real agenda is here. I have a hard time believing that taxes are the issue, although raising their spectre does make it personal. All of us want to have some say about where our hard-earned dollars get spent and I suspect for many people living in the farm belt this is a particularly sensitive issue, given the role government and big business plays in their lives. Talking about taxes is a sure-fire way to get attention, and insinuating that scarce and badly needed money is being squandered on lesbian art is a sure-fire way to fan the flame of homophobia. Homosexuality becomes yet again the target and scapegoat for a thinly veiled process of political maneuvering. Implicit in these articles is the message that the *wrong* people are in government and when election time comes around you can replace them with the *right* people.

The authors, and by extension, the magazines they write for, offer an authoritarian and one-dimensional view of homosexuality that fits their own right-wing ideology. Readers are given very little information and are encouraged to identify with these views by the assumption of implicit agreement with them, because the homophobic point of view is the only one offered. These arti-

was. That "as I recall" thing had me going. I would indeed do anything she wanted. First I would find out what she wanted and then I would do it.

I think I knew it was Halifax by these thoughts running through my head. No one else has quite this effect on me.

She was still reading.

Yes, she was more familiar all the time, but I needed a sign to make my move.

I waited for it, knowing it would come.

"Good book?"

It was Halifax. Undoubtedly. Who else would come up behind me like that? Who else would say to a famous visiting lecturer so obviously engrossed in high thoughts—"Good book?" She had no manners.

"I'm hungry," I said. "Do you want to go to the lounge?" I hadn't been there, but I knew there was one. There's always some kind of little room in the library basement, with vending machines and bright lights and yucky tables.

cles are legitimized by their tone of authority and by the covert implication that they speak from the only possible moral viewpoint, ultimately backed by a particularly homophobic God himself.

Until people are given truthful, respectful, and balanced reportage about queers and our lives, attitudes will remain frozen in fearful, hateful, and manipulative points of view. Playing on people's fears of identified minorities is an age-old strategy for grabbing power. Those who designate one group as the *bad* people, as opposed to the larger group of *good* people, are able to stream any number of social and economic woes together as being the fault of the (bad) oppressed minority group.

We don't have to look far back in history to see to what extremes scapegoating can lead. It is incumbent on all of us to learn how propaganda and manipulation work and to do what we can to protect ourselves and others from this form of mistreatment and social control.

AGAINST THE LAW:
SEX VERSUS THE QUEEN

Feminists won a stunning victory in February when Canada's Supreme Court ruled that obscenity is to be defined by the harm it does to women's pursuit of equality . . . The ruling has the support of most women's groups in Canada, where the free-speech tradition is not as dominant as it is in the U.S.; as a result, feminist debate on pornography is less intense.

—MS. MAGAZINE[1]

Confessional

PERSIMMON: I can't believe I read the whole thing. I'm just not that kind of girl. But it's true. I read the entire hit parade of recent Canadian anti-porn rulings, starting with Butler v. Her Majesty the Queen, and all its satellite documents—summary, majority decision (a mighty document, weighing in at 64 pages), minority concurrence, factums by LEAF and the B.C. Civil Liberties Association. Plus the Hayes decision, the Paris decision, and R. v. Ronish.

I am not a big reader of legal documents, god knows. They have this particular writing style that seems to have been developed to keep lawyers employed and the rest of us in the dark. But once I got into it, it had a strange fascination. Kind

1. "Canada: Anti-Pornography Breakthrough in the Law," *Ms. Magazine* (27 May 1992), p. 14.

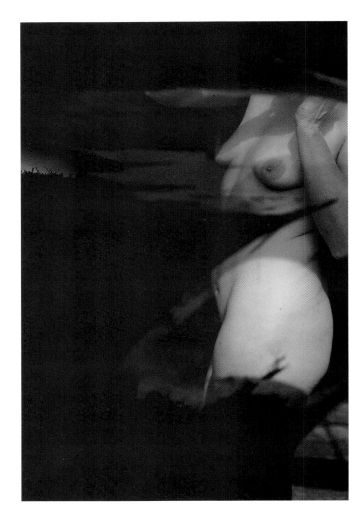

Do you

notice

my white skin and unbroken

limbs?

"Okay. Bring your book."

Hers was in her hand—*Veronica Digest.* Mine was an anthology of feminist writings about pornography. Off we went to the elevator, down three floors, along a musty corridor lined with books. I bought an apple. She bought a chocolate bar and a Coke.

"I know this great place on this floor where we can eat this stuff and even talk out loud and no one will know," she said.

More musty corridors. Shelves of books

stretched into the darkness on either side. She flicked on lights along the way. They were on timers. Hardly anyone came down here.

I began to know what she wanted. What I had promised.

Miraculously, there was a space with a padded bench at the end of our trek. To sit and rest with your book, I guessed. As I looked down where we had come I could already see the first lights she had switched on switching themselves off. She was brave as ever, tough, hard to get,

of like watching *Twin Peaks*. Weird, stupid, frustrating, and addictive, all at once.

So this is me, ranting my way through the labyrinth of porn law.

I owe a big debt to Agnes Huang, my source, my co-addict: for bringing me document after document; for being the only other person I know who reads this stuff; for our long, twisted discussions; and for disagreeing with me so profoundly and interestingly.

Whose victory

The Canadian Supreme Court ruling known as the Butler decision changes the definition of obscenity from a morals-based one to a harm-based one. Sexual imagery is now banned because it's believed to cause harm rather than because it offends the community's moral standards. The issues raised by this ruling are not unique. They are issues that come up again and again in discussions about censorship.

The Butler decision was backed by many feminists (though not by the overwhelming majority implied in the *Ms.* article, and not without intense opposition from many other feminists). Among the active supporters were women from the Legal, Education and Action Fund (LEAF), who were official interveners in the case, trying to get a ruling that recognized sexism rather than sex as the problem area in porn.

I recognize the good intentions of the women who backed Butler, but it seems like the reason it passed with such ease is because it *was* and *is* easily co-opted into a right-wing anti-sex, anti-gay, and anti-feminist agenda. Despite some feminist window dressing, it is the same old anti-porn law that's intended to suppress sexual expression, not sexism.

The Butler decision defines obscenity as "images of sex with violence or sex which degrades or dehumanizes any of the participants." But who gets to decide what is violent, dehumanizing, and degrading? Our friends the police? Our friends the courts? Our friends the Customs agents? How can the wording be

smart as a whip. But she wanted me here. She wanted me to live up to my promise and she was going to make me figure it out.

"So what are you reading?" she asked. Ever the college student.

"About pornography and optical appropriation," I said.

"What?"

"I mean, I'm looking at *Schaulust* and Freudian analysis, castration anxiety," I said.

"What?"

"You know, the phantom phallus, the gender masquerade."

"Okay, I'm impressed, but you need a shot of reality. Like, what's this got to do with me?"

"I'm not sure I can do justice to Odenso's thesis," I said. "I'm only halfway through the article."

"Lame answer," she said, looking at me sideways. "I notice you've put a lot of exclamation marks in the margins."

She knows why, I thought, but I wasn't going to give her that.

specific enough or vague enough to prevent mainstream authorities from using the law to target people who challenge their values?

A look at the walls of DRAWING THE LINE is enough to tell me that there are deep differences of interpretation within my own community. And I certainly don't trust the cops, courts, and Customs agents to be making those decisions. The policy of Canada Customs, in written law as well as in practice, is that anal penetration is degrading and dehumanizing. Always. No context, no nothing. This affects AIDS education materials as well as arts and entertainment sex. And although many lawyers have argued that Butler's emphasis on harm rather than explicitness means that Canada Customs should no longer consider anal penetration grounds for seizure, their policy hasn't changed.

As the Supreme Court stated in Butler, there's no proof that pornography causes harm. The "scientific evidence" is contradictory.

> While a direct link between obscenity and harm to society may be difficult to establish, it is reasonable to presume that exposure to an image bears a causal relationship to changes in attitudes and beliefs.
>
> —BUTLER V. THE QUEEN[2]

2. Justice John Sopinka, Majority decision, Supreme Court of Canada, Donald Butler v. Her Majesty the Queen, 1992.

And it does sound reasonable. Especially when you apply it to some theoretical Other Person who is ready to swallow down bad images and spit out bad behaviour. But what about you? What about your best friend? What about anti-porn feminists who have spent a lot of time researching pornography? I know if I were locked up in a room watching sexist porn for months on end, it wouldn't turn me into a rapist. Bored, yes. Violent, no.

It's more complicated than cause and effect. Living in a culture that's saturated with demeaning pictures of women is both an effect of sexism and one of the ways in which sexism is perpetuated.

But I don't think that explicitly sexual pictures harm women more than pic-

---

"And what are you reading?" I countered, as if I didn't know.

"Well, I'm looking at Archie comics as places where young gay people find role models. I'm trying to find episodes where Ethel shows her lesbianism, and where Jughead shows his gayness, and then trace in what decades the most gay strips were written, and when the homophobic ones were, and what messages kids get. I think it relates to discussions of the mutability of sexual identity in a quirky sort of way."

"Do you do this just to bug me?"

"Do what?" She was all wide eyed and innocent.

I noticed the lights were going out around us. We were sitting in the last circle of light. I had a vision of her desire for me, here, in this light, watched by books, the air silent and musty, at the heart of the beast, our sex at the centre. She wanted me and I had promised. There was no mistaking the look in her eyes, so strong I could play with it.

"Shouldn't we go now?" I teased her

"Oh, no need," she said quickly. Her breath was

tures that aren't explicit. In fact, since soft-core sexism permeates our society so thoroughly on an everyday level, I see its cumulative effect as *more* harmful. But the feminist strategy around non-explicit sexist imagery has rarely if ever been censorship. We have focussed on education, boycotts, lobbying, direct action protests, and the production of alternative imagery. Why the difference?

The way the law is currently written, brutal images of sexualized violence against women are acceptable if there's no nudity or actual sexual contact, whereas if their clothes are off, all it takes is the slightest implication of violence for it to run up against Butler. This doesn't make sense. It doesn't seem like a feminist victory.

That's the problem with trying to do a feminist rewrite of porn laws—they're already steeped in conservative moral values and an analysis of sexuality that is profoundly anti-woman. Many conservative politicians welcome a bit of feminist jargon to give a little cosmetic facelift to old legislation. Other politicians are floundering between two radically different world-views in the same piece of legislation and the result is a mishmash of unclear concepts and vague language which can be interpreted in wildly different ways.

Whatever we wear, wherever we go

Recently, a local newspaper quoted Valerie Harper talking about a Rape Treatment Centre she's involved with in Santa Monica, California. She was reported as saying, "There were more raped and brutalized women seeking help at the centre in March than ever before, and I think certain people in the entertainment world have to be aware that what they're doing has an impact . . . For her own personal advancement, Madonna has promoted images of herself manacled and chained in bed and similar poses. It's terribly irresponsible."[3]

Oh come on! So Madonna is responsible for all those rapes? Is this the new rape defense in the USA—"Madonna made me do it!"? Whatever happened to men being held responsible for their own actions? The shift in assigning the re-

3. Marilyn Beck and Stacy Jenel Smith, "Madonna Cited in Rape Film," *Vancouver Province*, 20 April 1993, p. B7.

coming faster. We both knew. "This light's not on a timer."

I looked at her. She was a stranger. I held Birgit Odenso.

"Anything . . ." she ventured, that word that could catch me anytime.

I looked up.

" . . . else you want to talk about?" She was shameless. "Anything you want?"

I shook my head. The gig was up. But I was going to make her say it. I waited.

"There's things I want," she said finally. "You said it was for sex. This is sex."

I looked at her—that hand, that hand. I would do anything. "Well? What things? What do you want?" I said.

She was silent.

I held my book, a talisman, Birgit.

I stood up, took off my pants, sat back down. She watched, mute.

Oh Birgit, I thought, make her fuck me again. I'll do anything. This is what she wants.

sponsibility for rape to sexual imagery, rather than actual people, is chilling. To say that a woman shouldn't explore her sexuality (the hard parts as well as the sweet parts) because it might incite men to rape is an old, old line.

There was a court case in Minnesota where the judge let a rapist off with a light sentence because the girl he raped in the hall of her high school was "provocatively dressed." Both this ruling and the accusations against Madonna are rooted in the theory that men are helpless to control themselves when inflamed by scantily clothed women (in pictures or in the flesh). I don't buy it, and I don't buy anti-porn legislation that perpetuates this kind of boys-will-be-boys-they-can't-control-themselves-so-we-have-to-control-what-they-see thing. Seeing a picture of something doesn't give you the right to do it in real life, whether it's a TV murder or a video rape. That's not a difficult concept. Men can grasp that.

Women make sex
Neither the Butler decision nor the LEAF factum to the Supreme Court as an intervener in Butler differentiates between sexual images produced by men and those produced by women, or between fantasy and reality, or coercion and consent. Women as producers or consumers of sexual imagery are invisible. We exist only as victims of pornography. The word fantasy is never mentioned. Consent is deemed irrelevant. This makes for problems.

Pornography is assumed to be made by men and for men. Sexual images by and for women are never mentioned. It's such a familiar erasure of our lives. It leads to a law where what is assumed to be true about men is by default assumed to be true about women. A *Penthouse* portrayal of a woman in bondage and a woman's portrayal of herself in bondage are seen as the same thing. There is no difference between a tired old view of the Subordinated Other, and a vulnerable self-exploration.

The vinyl bench cold on my butt. My vulva would betray me, hot and wet, I knew it.

Her breath fast and sharp, eyes glittering, powerless to stop me. I touched myself.

Hot and wet and slippery. Clichés in my head. I'll do anything. You're so sexy. Oh baby oh baby oh baby. Oh please please please.

My hardened clit made me shake so I couldn't hold the book. Her desire, my promise, my desire.

She watched.

I felt her tongue before I saw her move. She was kneeling in front of me, soft tongue, sharp teeth, strong lips. In the last circle of light, dark stacks, slippery vinyl bench.

"Oh baby oh baby oh baby I'll do anything I'll do anything for you. I'll . . . do . . . anything."

Her hand under my shirt squeezing my nipple, pain making me gasp, her tongue on my theory. "Anything, anything."

"Really?" That hand, hard and fast, driving me, banging again and again against the wall, my head swimming the universe unfolding, who cares who

Presumed

homosexual unless specified

otherwise

sees? The books shadowy on grey shelves, who
cares? I'll do what you want, just ask, I'll beg you
the light   the dark   the bench   I'll do anything
I'll do anything   I'll do anything . . .
   "Liar."

> Pornography is made to produce male sexual excitement, erection and masturbation through the harms outlined above. It is not made to further any search for truth.
>
> —LEAF FACTUM TO THE SUPREME COURT[4]

4. File No. 22191, Supreme Court of Canada, Donald Butler v. Her Majesty the Queen, Factum of the intervener Women's Legal, Education and Action Fund.

Women as self-defining sexual subjects have been invisible or punished in Euro-American culture. There's a lot of scope for a search for truth here. Women have many arguments with each other about sex. Many questions are raised, and we're not always happy with each other's answers. But surely we don't want to give the patriarchal legal system the right to silence our disagreements. Did anti-porn feminists really intend this law to ban the exploration of women's own sexual imagery? Sure we get furious with each other about issues of sexual representation, but if feminists turn to the men of the courts to settle our disputes, we are forgetting who our enemies really are.

The reality of fantasy

There is an incredible difference between fantasy (and the acting out of fantasies) and something really happening.

I've never heard a woman say she enjoyed any part of being raped. But I've heard many women say they enjoy the fantasy of being raped. Sometimes a woman will be turned on by the exact thing that, in real life, was her most painful and traumatic experience. Where do these fantasies come from? Some people say that whatever is hidden or forbidden becomes desirable, so married women fantasize adultery and lesbians fantasize sex with men, and so on. Other people say these fantasies are self-destructive replays of internalized sexism and past pain that would go away if we worked them out on an emotional/psychological level. Other people say these fantasies are a way of working out past pain by replaying it in a context where we are in control. Other people say, "What does it matter, I'm not hurting anyone!"

I don't think that one analysis of sexual fantasies is adequate to explain all fantasies of all women for all time.

> . . . pornography lies about women and their sexuality; for example, that women live to be raped, love to be hurt, and are fulfilled by abuse. Pornography silences women's expression and inhibits truth seeking . . .
>
> —LEAF FACTUM

The problem with this statement is that its makes no distinction between sexual fantasy and reality. Women's truth-seeking is inhibited if we deny that *some* women *do* love to be hurt, that they are *aroused* by rape fantasies, *enjoy* acts that in other contexts would be abuse. We need to look at where we really are, in all its complexity, not pretend that we're all too nice to have these feelings. The fear seems to be that if we talk about it (write about it, make images of it), some men will take that as license to hurt, rape, and abuse women.

I expect men to know the difference between fantasy and reality. I expect men (and women) to be able to hear a woman say that she sometimes likes to be tied up and beaten *in the time and place and by the person of her choice,* and not think that means they can do it any time to any woman.

If some men don't understand the difference between yes and no, or not right now, or not with you, it's time they learned. I don't accept laws that believe those excuses. I'm sick and tired of having to watch my ass (and my art) so I don't "provoke" male violence.

> Consent cannot save materials that otherwise contain degrading or dehumanizing scenes. Sometimes the very appearance of consent makes the depicted acts even more degrading and dehumanizing.
>
> —BUTLER V. THE QUEEN

BOSTON

"Got some time?" he said.

"Absolutely not," I answered in my best fuck-off tone of voice.

He was there, waiting outside the front door to the theatre, when I came out after the performance. There was supposed to be a cab waiting, he must have signalled it on. I didn't need this, I really didn't need this.

He leaned against the door frame, blocking my exit. Beneath the cotton shirt I could see the well-defined muscles of someone who spends a lot of time at the gym. He wasn't a jock, though. He looked like the type of guy who would hang out at a bookstore or a cafe. A musician or writer. The "sensitive type." Definitely not a faggot, though. Not looking at me like that.

"Have we met?" I asked him. "You look familiar."

If women are powerless victims, we don't have the power to consent or refuse. And sometimes we don't. Sometimes we are physically or economically constrained so that consent is meaningless. But sometimes we *do* have the power to consent, and if what we seek out and consent to is not what other people would have us do, it is still our consent that we are exercising. That power to consent doesn't only apply to lesbians. Some straight women fully consent to being tied up, hit, and fucked by a man. It's incredibly disrespectful for other women (and men) to pretend such acts only happen if women are physically, economically, or emotionally forced. Yes, there are vast gulfs of inequality (and not just between men and women), but it's condescending to deny that we very often have power, choice, and the sense to use them.

Butler talks about consent only as "the appearance of consent" and not in terms of the huge difference it makes to our experience of an interaction. Surely we don't need to choose between acknowledging our power and acknowledging when we are victimized. Consent is real and it's crucial. It's the difference between giving ourselves and being robbed.

Porn again

That pornography causes harm is such a sweeping statement. How does pornography *actually function?* Is it the same everywhere, for everyone? Are there differences from community to community? Cultural and class differences? Urban/rural differences? How does gay and lesbian porn function within *our* communities? Does it cause harm? How do geographical, cultural, racial, and class differences affect the ways that porn functions in various gay and lesbian communities?

These questions are considered irrelevant in Canada now. The Butler decision has enshrined the concept of a national community standard. This means that there is no recognition of differing views on obscenity from place to place,

"Yeah, we've met," he said. He gave a small half-smile. "I'm a fan. I never miss a show when you women are around."

He did look like someone I knew but I couldn't place him. "You women" obviously meant dykes. I knew about guys like this, they sometimes hang out in the dyke bars. Someone told me once that quite a few of them are retired cops. They usually don't talk to the women, they just sit in the corner, nurse beers and watch. I couldn't figure this guy though, he wasn't that kind of pervert. Too *nice* looking, immaculately dressed, sexy and smart-assed.

"I thought you might like to go for a drive," he said. "Get in a little sight-seeing before you fly home tomorrow, maybe go for dinner."

How did he know that I was leaving tomorrow? Had we mentioned it during the show? I suppose we must have, but I wasn't certain.

This was a waste of time. Sure I wanted to see Boston, sure I wanted to go for a drive, I even wanted sex, but not with this guy. I'd had someone

culture to culture. It also means that materials created by and for the gay and lesbian communities will not be judged by the standards of the gay and lesbian communities, but by the standards of an imagined national mainstream of Canadians. The door is wide open for homophobia.

When the Butler decision was being argued, many lesbians and gay men spoke out against it. It wasn't a case of us wanting "special rights" for our sexual images. It was a case of knowing our history. We knew that anti-porn laws are applied unequally, against gays and lesbians. We knew that, no matter what LEAF's intentions, there was a good chance of Butler being used against us by the courts and the cops—people with a proven track record of homophobia. And we were right, as a look at some recent applications of Butler show.

A few days after the Butler decision came down, the police busted Glad Day Books in Toronto for selling the noncommercial, lesbian-produced sex magazine *Bad Attitude*. There was nothing in the seized magazine that isn't in Madonna's book *Sex*.[5] The court judged *Bad Attitude* obscene, but *Sex* has never even been hassled. Money changes everything. Being straight helps too.

In another recent decision, in Ontario, Judge Hayes ruled that a group of soft-core gay sex magazines seized from Glad Day were obscene. Here's an example of his reasoning:

> *Advocate Men:* This is a magazine of explicit pictures of nude males and stories of explicit casual sexual encounters relating to oral and anal sex. The description and activities are degrading and without any human dimension. The dominant characteristic is the undue exploitation of sex. I find it to be obscene.
> —GLAD DAY BOOKSHOP V. CANADA[6]

5. Madonna, *Sex* (New York: Warner Books, 1992).

6. Hayes J., Glad Day Bookshop Inc. v. Canada (Deputy Minister of National Revenue, Customs and Excise—M.N.R.) Ontario Court (General Division), 1992.

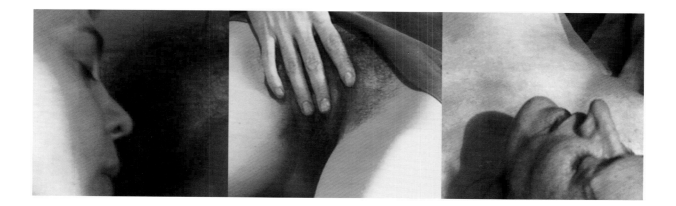

Anti-porn feminists did nothing to guard against such mis-use of Butler. In fact, LEAF used gay male porn to argue their case. LEAF's lawyer in the Butler case was quoted in *Ms. Magazine* as saying:

> How did we do it? We showed them the porn—and among the seized videos were some horrifically violent and degrading gay movies. We made the point that the abused men in these films were being treated like women—and the judges got it. Otherwise men can't put themselves in our shoes."[7]

7. "Canada: Anti-Pornography Breakthrough in the Law," (see note 1), p. 14.

She seems so unconcerned with how her arguments may be playing into the homophobia of these judges, so indifferent to the possible consequences for gay men and lesbians, so willing to lump all sexual imagery together with no knowledge of its functioning in particular communities.

The fact that that some gay porn may look similar to straight porn is not proof that it is used in the same ways, with the same social effects.

It's a common mistake to assume that what goes on in the dominant groups in society is also what happens in all other groups. Sometimes I assume that how things look to me, as a middle-class person, is how things *are*. It's called classism. I can deny it, or I can own up to it and learn from my mistakes. Likewise homophobia.

> . . . LEAF submits that much of the subject pornography of men for men, in addition to abusing some men in the ways that it is more common to abuse women through sex, arguably contributes to abuse and homophobia as it normalizes male sexual aggression generally.
>
> —LEAF FACTUM

This statement takes a certain analysis of heterosexual porn and lays it over gay male porn, ignoring the particularities of fag sex. Gay s/m "normalizes" male

else on my mind all week. I'd been sure Halifax would show up, was counting on it. She'd gotten to me, damn her, and now where was she?

I looked at the man standing in front of me; there was something sweet about him. He was just standing there waiting for me to tell him again to fuck off, looking at me like he knew how I was feeling. Shit, I wanted to talk to someone, needed to tell someone . . .

"How about the park, right over there?" he said, pointing across the street. "I'll buy you a coffee and we can stroll through the grounds, we can talk."

I didn't think I'd be in any danger. I could have called out to my friends, but something stopped me, and whatever that something was, it was confusing the hell out of me. I was slightly attracted to this guy and that felt weird, really weird. Then it occurred to me—what She would think if she saw me with him, and I felt angry and reckless.

"Okay," I said, "a quick coffee, let's go." He

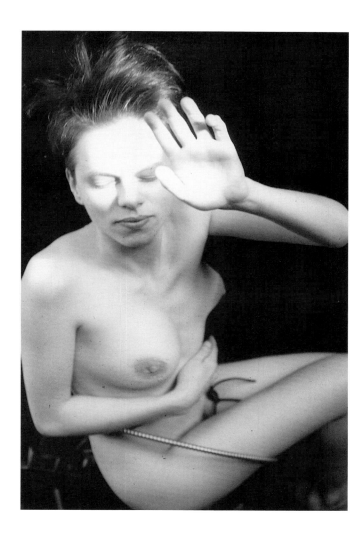

Maybe

I'm exactly what

you think

I am.

took my arm and maneuvered me onto the busy sidewalk. I felt like laughing at the thought of myself strolling down the street arm in arm with this man. An hour ago I was on the stage as the visiting artist, the lesbian sex star extolling the virtues of down-and-dirty lesbian smut and here I was passing for straight. This was twisted and I almost enjoyed it.

We strolled in silence. I couldn't think of a thing to say to this stranger. It was enough to walk and try to sort out the riot of confused emotion that

was starting to percolate inside me. Now that I was thinking of Her I couldn't stop. I saw her as she appeared to me the last time we'd met, the coy academic, and that first time in Halifax, and the mystery of Sydney. Every encounter had left its mark on me and the harder I resisted her, the deeper in I went. I started to ache with longing and the more I thought about her, the worse it got.

My companion slipped his arm around me and I felt myself relax into the comfort of her embrace, except it wasn't her. It was this guy and what

sexual *submission* just as much as aggression. Gay s/m porn is frequently from the point of view of the bottom. This makes sense, since the majority of s/m fags switch roles, with a preference for being bottom. Their imagery isn't constructed with a static assumption that the viewer will identify with (and copy) the aggressor. The viewer is more likely to slip back and forth, identifying with either or both roles, depending on how the image intersects with his particular interests, desires, and self-image at that moment.

Women on top

Another point of view that is totally disregarded by this analysis is the whole genre of het/erotica, where a woman is the aggressor and a man is submissive. It's primarily aimed at heterosexual men who identify with the submissive role. What does this have to do with inequality or violence against women? Does anyone really think that women who see this stuff will get violent? It's actually the most common form of het s/m;[8] why wasn't it discussed? Perhaps because it doesn't fit the model where the (male) viewer identifies with the top, the bottom is a (female) victim, and consent is meaningless. It complicates things.

Canadian anti-porn law doesn't acknowledge complications of gender and sexuality. Several rulings since the Butler decision have specifically stated that gender doesn't matter when discussing harm. What matters is the judges' idea of what constitutes "human dignity" and "real human relationships." This isn't what LEAF was after. Images that have no relationship to LEAF's analysis of harm and equality are defined as degrading and dehumanizing. Our feminist victory is easily broken down into mainstream moralism in the end.

Protection racket

Direct physical violence to real people is inflicted in order to make some pornography, particularly visual pornography. Some women are coerced into pornography and sexually assaulted so that pornog-

8. Anne McClintock, "Maid to Order," in *Dirty Looks,* ed. Pamela Church Gibson and Roma Gibson (London: BFI Publishing, 1993), 211-12.

the fuck was I doing?

"Don't do that," I said, shaking him off and immediately regretting it. "Look, I've got to go. You're an okay dude but I'm not into it, I'm a dyke and I miss my girlfriend." Girlfriend? Could I even call her that? How about 'fuck-buddy'? My serial one-night stand? My magical mistress? I'll give her one thing, she defied categorization. My no-name friend who had my number whether I liked it or not. And mostly I liked it. Craved it, yearned for it, ate my heart out for it, and despaired of not having it.

She fed me my habit on a silver spoon and I lapped it up like honey.

"Where is your girlfriend?" my companion of the moment asked me, breaking into my reverie. I looked at him and he was looking back at me intently. "Somewhere else, I don't know, far away, probably," I answered, feeling miserable. "I never know where she is or when I'll see her again. It was crazy fun at first, but now it feels messed up, like I'm out of control with it. She shows up when she wants to," I felt tears coming and I struggled to

raphy can be made of them . . . Pornography which is made from assaults and which exacerbates the injury of those assaults is no more worthy of protection as expression than are the assaults themselves.

—LEAF FACTUM

Right on! It should be right in there with the other laws that make sure people don't profit from coercive acts. But the Butler decision doesn't refer to situations of *actual* violence and coercion at all. Reality is ignored, fantasy is punished. Maybe they figured that if they ban sexual images that *look* violent or degrading, it would guarantee that nothing bad happened in the *making* of those pictures. All I can say is, those judges have probably never been sex models. What happens on a shoot and what the viewer sees in the pictures are very, very different.

Some women are raped and abused in the making of sexual images. Some of the resulting images appear to be of "vanilla sex." But it's still coercion. Much of the porn that Linda Lovelace acted in featured straight vanilla sex (as described in her powerful book *Ordeal*).[9] But she was violated in the process. She was being raped, but it doesn't always "show" in the videos.

9. Linda Lovelace, *Ordeal* (Berkeley: Berkeley Publishing, 1987).

Lack of clarity about the importance of consent and the difference between a picture and real life leads to a judgement that ignores women in her situation.

But let's get real—this law isn't about protecting sex workers. Do any anti-porn rulings protect women in the sex industry? Do anti-porn laws give those women more control or make their working conditions safer?

Sex workers are particularly vulnerable to violence in this country. Prostitutes have been fighting for safer working conditions for a long time, and one thing that their organizations seem to agree on is that anti-prostitution laws don't make them safer. Anti-prostitution laws put their lives even further at risk.

In Canada, Bill C-49, the 1985 law that made it easier to prosecute sex workers, has led to a horrifying increase in murders of street-involved women. Assaults have also sky-rocketed. This is in part because police have driven women

keep them at bay. "I don't even know her goddamned name." The lunacy of this comment almost made me want to laugh. Why was I telling all this to a guy I'd never met before?

"What's *your* name?" I asked my companion. He didn't answer my question but nodded in sympathy and I was touched by his sweet and quiet solace.

I let him take my hand and lead me toward a fountain. It was getting late and the square was deserted. He leaned against a stone wall, placed his hands on my shoulders and gently pulled me toward him. I watched myself go into his arms with a mixture of revulsion, fascination, and dread. This was a *man,* had I completely lost my head? And then suddenly, with absolutely no warning, I was with Her again, it was her mouth I was tasting, her heart beating against mine, her desire spinning me into orbit. He spoke then, and she disappeared.

"You're beautiful," he murmured, "tell me you want it, tell me how much you want it." I barely heard him. I didn't want *it,* I wanted Her. I ran my hands over her ass and pulled her against me. I

from their old areas of business, where there were well-developed networks for watching out for each other. They must now work on streets that are often ill lit and isolated. There is constant police harassment. It's harder for women to work as independents without the protection of a man. They certainly can't rely on the legal system to protect them.

The more illegal their work is, the more they're driven into dark corners, the more their lives are at risk. What many prostitutes are demanding is the decriminalization of prostitution, so that they can organize for better working conditions. Laws and attitudes that stigmatize sex workers put their lives at risk.

It's so stupidly typical that the effects of porn are argued and laws are passed without the input of women who work in the pornography business. It isn't up to Kiss & Tell or LEAF or any other outside group to decide what women working in the commercial porn business need. Women within the industry are best placed to decide what legislation, what economic changes, and what support from other women would be beneficial.

The good parts

Yes, Butler is flawed, Butler is vague, Butler is bad. I wish we could drop it in the ocean and start again. But Butler is what we've got and it's going to be with us for a long time. We can't sulk about it forever. We've got to try to get the best possible interpretations of that vague thing.

For all its faults, the Butler decision may turn out to be better than the previous approach to porn legislation. The good part is the result of LEAF's attempt to get the court to look at the issue of equality. Throughout their factum, LEAF argues for anti-porn laws that are based on promoting women's equality. It's basically an argument against sexualized hate literature. I may disagree with some anti-porn feminists about where the lines are drawn between interesting sexual exploration, dumb bozo sexist imagery, and actual hate literature, but I don't disagree with laws that defend "historically disadvantaged groups" from hate

gloried in her muscular body, the tight jeans, the smell of her leather jacket, the man's scent she was wearing. I bit her neck and heard him moan. He lifted me up on a shallow ledge and her hands were under my skirt, I felt the cold stone on my naked skin. I undid the button on his jeans as I felt the hard bulge underneath. I wanted her so much I could hardly breathe.

"I was so afraid you wouldn't make it," I whispered. There was no answer but I felt a warm mouth exactly where I liked it best, a mouth like no other mouth. I started sliding and spiralling down toward that place where she and I had met so many times before, that place where perfect sense could be made of the world, where heat and light reigned absolute. I wanted to call out to her but there was no name to call. "Who are you?" "Who are you?" I wanted to scream but my voice was inaudible as my body responded again and again to her insistent caress. After an age she was there, inside me. I felt the first thrust, the second, the third, I was bursting with joy. We rode the startled

propaganda. Especially in today's climate, I value laws that recognize the inequality of our society and attempt to promote change.

There are people on both sides of the pornography/censorship debate who argue their position by presenting a ridiculously oversimplified version of the opposing position and then shooting it down. This may make cheap points for their side, but it does nothing to further our understanding of these complex issues. It's hard enough figuring this stuff out without that kind of posturing.

Some people say LEAF's position on equality is that if porn is banned, women will be equal, which is obviously ridiculous. That is *not* LEAF's position. LEAF says that sexist imagery is *one* of the many factors contributing to women's inequality. They say that only by fighting on many fronts will women's equality be won. I feel that another contributing factor is the suppression of women's own imagery, whether by poverty, by lack of access to tools and distribution, or by censorship laws. A law based on equality arguments could be turned around to protect the sexual self-expression of women and other marginalized groups.

The Supreme Court gutted LEAF's equality language in the actual decision, but to the extent that it's still there, it gives us a possible place to stand. It gives us a basis on which to defend work that offends "community standards of morality" but can be seen as an empowering exploration of traditionally silenced groups. That's certainly not how most judges have been interpreting Butler, but the possibility is there for defending dissident work, rather than having it be the first target of anti-porn laws.

Different alliances
One of the (many) problems with how polarized the anti-porn and anti-censorship camps have been, is that we forget how much common ground we actually have, and don't acknowledge valid criticisms and concerns when they're brought up by "the other side." We have major disagreements that are nowhere

horses, on and on we sped as time and space conspired to stop, did stop, and everything became distilled into one suspended moment.

That is when I saw Her. One utterly insane moment of perfect clarity and I saw who she really was. I laughed aloud at the simplicity of her ruse.

She was leaning against me, her face hidden in the folds of my jacket. I felt like crying and laughing, ecstasy and grief all rolled into one tight ball lodged in my throat, my throbbing cunt. I felt like murdering her. "Bitch," I murmured as I

watched her shoulders shake with ill-disguised laughter. "You'd better watch your ass, girl. I know who you are and I know where to find you," I whispered. He looked up then and I stared into the face of a stranger.

near being settled, but that shouldn't blind us to areas where we could work together. The fight against right-wing interpretations of anti-porn laws is not a place where anti-porn and anti-censorship feminists need to be divided.

A year after the Butler decision, members of LEAF met with anti-censorship feminists in Toronto to discuss their differences. From all reports it was an angry meeting, but they came out of it with a joint press release that denounced the discriminatory applications of Butler against lesbians, gay men, and sex workers.

If you support anti-porn laws, you don't have to support discriminatory actions made in their name. If you feel that censorship gives needed protection to women, you can still fight against anti-gay applications of those laws. It's a failure of imagination to view this situation as a necessary trade-off, where you have to decide whose rights are more important to protect.

We can argue about whether Butler was a good idea or not, but what are we going to *do* about the ways it's applied that are clearly discriminatory? Homophobia is not the only issue here. What are the class biases of our anti-porn laws? Are the laws enforced equally against middle-class artists and sex workers? (No way!) What cultural biases, sexist biases, racist biases are being enforced? Our job now is to fight for the best possible interpretations of Butler, interpretations not based on homophobia, classism, racism, or conservative moral values hiding behind feminist language.

There are many hopeful signs that the polarization between anti-porn and anti-censorship feminists is lessening. We have disagreements. We may argue, get mad, hang up on each other. But we aren't each other's enemies. We have a lot of common ground and many areas where we can work together. We'd better get on with it.

QUESTIONING CENSORSHIP

For me, freedom of speech and censorship exist within the discourse of power. To censor requires the power to impose one's views, ideologies, realities, and the power to silence others. How can I have freedom of speech when I am continually silenced by sexism, racism, and homophobia?

—AGNES HUANG[1]

Ban censorship

LIZARD: I cannot make sense of the censorship debates. I mean, I know where I stand on certain things, but in the context of the censorship discussion as it is framed, my stands are contradictory. I try to make everything go together and end up going around in circles, worrying at the same arguments in the same succession.

I'm sick of it. The word "censorship" should be banned. It is too loaded, and is used to mean too many different things.

Feminist activists use "censorship" in a particular political discourse, namely the discussion of sexual representation. It has a sort of political shorthand to it, and "anti-censorship feminist" carries with it a host of political positions. It puts you on one side of a once impossibly sharp fence.

1. Agnes Huang, letter to authors, January 1994.

We in Kiss & Tell are anti-censorship feminists by default. As lesbian art makers, we have no choice: our desires and our art have put us here. Our culture is continually silenced, our sexuality erased. Our work has been seized, refused, banned. And it is only anti-censorship activists who seem to care.

But being anti-censorship is twisted around in sordid ways. Neo-Nazis and Holocaust deniers lie to glorify the most repressive and brutally *pro*-censorship regime of recent European history, and they defend themselves by saying they are *anti*-censorship. Politics may make strange bedfellows, but I will not ally myself with these people. That's clear enough for me.

PERSIMMON: And then there are our alliances with liberals. I was at a forum recently where a civil liberties activist spoke proudly about his organization's principles. His group, he said, believed so strongly in freedom of speech that they would defend society's rejects whom no one else would touch: homosexuals and Nazis. The way he talked had a whole row of lesbians flinching. And this guy is supposed to be on our side.

He was firmly against censorship, and painted a glowing picture of the alternative, a "free market of ideas" where all would join the fray of democratic debate, and theories that were racist and sexist and selfish and mean would eventually be seen for what they are, and be consigned to the rubbish heap of history.

The pure anti-censorship position is very appealing because it's so clear. It's the "just say no" approach. You don't have to make judgements and draw fine lines between this and that, and see all the ways it can backfire and figure out what to do about them. But when has the marketplace been free? And why haven't those ancient stereotypes hawked by hate mongers disappeared yet? The market isn't free, it's stacked against some of us. Until gay-bashing, synagogue-burning, and racist murders are a thing of the past, I'll keep supporting laws against hate-literature.

Does this put me on the pro-censorship side of the fence? According to

some civil libertarians it does. But it's a stupid fence. It cuts my life up in ways that don't make sense. What is ignored is power: who has it and who doesn't.

Strange ideas: opinion as censorship

PERSIMMON: Censorship is a word some people use every time someone disagrees with them, especially if that someone has made a political criticism of their work. For example, some people say, "If you call my work sexist/racist/homophobic/etc. you are censoring me."

Someone saying you shouldn't do something isn't the same as someone forcibly preventing you. Yes, criticism can be very painful to hear. Often when people have political criticisms of my work, I feel hurt, misunderstood, silenced. I feel like I never want to open my mouth again. But as you can see, here I am, opening my mouth. Criticism has not, in fact, silenced me.

People have a right to protest, and a right to a say in their own representation. I can't equate that with Canada Customs seizing books. Canada Customs has the power to stop hundreds of gay and lesbian books from coming into Canada, and they do. The homophobia implicit in their decisions is backed by a long history of laws, institutions, and social norms which discriminate against us. But when a lesbian group in Northampton, Massachusetts protested against DRAWING THE LINE, saying it promoted violence against women, they had neither the power of the state nor the power of social sanction to use against us. They were angry, they were protesting, but they were not censors.

SUSAN: Politically Correct, the very phrase sends my mind into paroxysms of confusion—oh what tangled webs we weave.

When I was a fresh-faced activist, back in the seventies, these words actually meant something. That is, I could count on them meaning a very specific thing, political ethics. Political correctness in those days was a useful teaching tool for young, naive, and politically inept newcomers like myself. It served as a method

HOMETOWN

Hometown, USA. As pinched and dry as ever. The same heat, the same dust, the same brown mountains closing in. The same low buildings under a new coat of made-up history. Kitty's Saloon, with its tired waitresses in Old West drag. Peso Pete's Western Souvenirs, with its window display of five-and-dime racism. Mac's Liquor. The Pinky Laundromat. Home. Coming back here was not a smart idea.

Any friends I once had in this place had all run, like I had run, as soon as they could scrape together bus fare to somewhere else. I had no relatives here who were still speaking to me. This was not a town that loved its lesbian daughters.

All I had was this dumb idea that since I was going to be a couple of hundred miles away in the state capital for a weekend conference on

of analysis, understanding, and consciousness raising that suggested possible attitude and behaviour changes. For example, "It's not politically correct to buy California grapes because farm workers are being exploited," or, "It's politically incorrect to use sexist slurs even if they were meant as a joke."

Later the words lost their gloss and progressive people dropped the phrase because it had taken on the additional meanings of political rigidity, dogma, and limitation. It seemed to have outlived its original usefulness. Political correctness became something to joke about, and in lesbian circles it also became something to react against. Many lesbians challenged the notion of political correctness as a way to extend boundaries and explore taboo territories. I can still remember when wearing lipstick was a rebellious act in lesbian/feminist circles, to say nothing about packing a dildo and the fine art of penetration. The thrills of being incorrect were sweet indeed.

So where has the Right been all these years and why the new spin on this term? Are they really so behind the times or am I missing something here?

It seems there is a lot of mileage to be gotten from twisting the meaning of this language around and using it as a verbal smart-bomb. A challenge to hate-literature suddenly becomes a threat to freedom of expression, or equity legislation becomes discrimination against white males. And all because of the repressive forces of political correctness? I hadn't realized that we had become such a threat. Nor could I have imagined that concepts that once spoke of integrity and fairness would be turned against us in such a lethal and transparently malicious way.

KISS & TELL: What does it mean these days to say someone is "politically correct"? Sometimes it means there's left-wing political content in their artwork. Sometimes it means they talk a lot about the importance of political art. Sometimes it means they trash all art that isn't political. Sometimes it means they don't laugh at sexist jokes. Sometimes it means they get mad at sexist jokes. Sometimes it means their use of language is nervously careful and spiked with

censorship, I might as well spend a few days visiting the land of my birth. To reconnect with my roots? To ponder my past? To buy an Authentic Western Shirt for only $12.98 plus tax?

I was staying at the Bucking Bronco Motel. It was like any motel anywhere. My room was small and barren and smelled like air conditioning. I was kept awake half the night by a pair of bucking broncos next door. They checked out in the morning looking fresh and rested and very pleased with themselves. I was *so* happy for them.

After I unglued my eyelids and unspiked my hair, I moseyed on down to the corner cafe for breakfast. The waitress brought me a cup of that watery stuff they think is coffee in the USA. It didn't work. When my breakfast special arrived, I asked for a cup of tea. Oh Canada. If you leave the tea bag in long enough you can get a reliable hit of caffeine as it eats away your stomach lining. She brought me presweetened ice tea. Back in the USA. How could I have forgotten so many of our quaint national customs?

I was just finishing my home fries when She

guilt. Sometimes it means they put down everyone who hasn't been educated in the same political language as they have. Sometimes it means they speak up when they think something's wrong.

The term "politically correct" is the right-wing popular culture counterpart of those great put-downs of the old Left, like "running dog lackey of the bourgeoisie." It's a name-calling term, vague and imprecise, a smear tactic rather than a concrete description of someone's actions or attitudes. When someone is called politically correct, it carries a host of unspoken implications, which may not apply to the actual situation in question.

It's a big crossover item—it's in gay and lesbian magazines as well as straight ones, and it's no longer useful. The term is used too often to trivialize dissent. If you call us politically correct, we don't know what you mean. At this point in time, given the constant use of the term in mainstream media, we'll probably think it means we're left-wing political artists and you don't think we should be, which is your tough luck. But it might be an important insight into ways that we behave which are really obnoxious. Why not drop the term and be clear about specific criticisms? Otherwise, we're just smearing each other with the right-wing's shit.

PERSIMMON: Why do I read the newspaper? It just drives me crazy. Like this little item from the front page of the *Vancouver Sun:* "Political correctness poses a greater threat to freedom of speech than any government undertaking, Supreme Court Justice John Sopinka said Thursday." [2] And he should know. He wrote the majority opinion in the Butler decision. Yes, that same Butler decision that has been applied so consistently against gay and lesbian materials. But never mind that! What you should really be worrying about is political correctness. Tell me more, Justice Sopinka!

" . . . he also warned that if judges are forced to work under constant fear of being rebuked for every action and utterance that falls from their bench, it 'may

2. Geoff Baker, "Judge's View: Political Correctness 'threat to free speech'," *Vancouver Sun,* 29 October 1993, p.1

walked in. Why am I even surprised any more?

"Howdy partner," she said with a wide cowboy grin.

"Don't," I said. "Just don't."

She parked her butt on the stool next to mine. "You're in a fun mood," she said.

"Try Disney World," I said.

The waitress brought her coffee, which she sipped with apparent relish.

"So, are you going to show me your old house and all that?" she asked.

"No."

"How about the reservoir where you first kissed Sally Stanley?"

"How do you know about that?"

"Oh, well . . . you hear things. She's working on a disabled dykes' newsletter in Chicago these days. Very tough gal, Sally."

"You're making that up!"

"Maybe so, maybe not. You'll never know, will you?" She tried the grin again. She was good, but no match for me and my evil mood.

result in decisions that are politically correct, but may not be legally and factually correct." The utterances alluded to include a particular series of wildly sexist remarks made by judges, in court, that some feminists saw as lacking in judicial impartiality.

The nerve of those women, rebuking our judges like that! Don't they know that judges are delicate creatures? They can't stand being rebuked, they just buckle under the strain. Yes, our legal system is in great danger. And our arts system too—it's already fallen, and lies helpless under the heel of the "politically correct"!

If all my information came from the mainstream media, I'd think that art today is wholly dominated by stern, self-righteous people of colour together with an army of shrill and simplistic white queers—as well as the occasional fat, middle-aged feminist. We run it all! It's amazing!

We have such power that we can silence anyone who disagrees with us! All art must conform to our rigid and narrow standards of political correctness! We control the galleries, the critics, the granting agencies! University administrators quake in fear and fall all over themselves to do our bidding! There are only a few brave and lonely souls who dare to lift their voices against the totalitarian rule of the politically correct. But at great personal risk, they *do* speak out, every day, in the *Vancouver Sun, Macleans, Newsweek,* the *New Yorker,* the *CBC,* the *Globe and Mail,* network TV, the *New York Times . . .*

But my delusions of grandeur are burst every time I put down the paper and look around me. We don't run the world. W. P. Kinsella[3] is still a best-seller. He hasn't been silenced by First Nations writers who suggest that they also deserve access to publishing, promotion, and distribution. White straight men still get more shows, more grants, more reviews.

It's not that things haven't changed. They have. Fifteen years ago I was one of the few openly lesbian students at my art school, and we were taught that political art is bad art. Nowadays, that same school has one or two arts-and-

3. W. P. Kinsella is a white Canadian writer who has been widely criticized by First Nations people for inaccurate and stereotypical portrayals of their cultures.

I paid the bill and left a tip for the waitress. It wasn't her fault.

Out on the street, the heat struck like a slap in the face. The sidewalk lurched under my feet but Her arm was around me, holding me up. I clung to her until the street stopped spinning.

Coming back here was not a smart idea.

When my lungs remembered how to breathe, she discreetly removed her arm from my waist. Don't scare the horses. We walked through downtown, all two blocks of it. Halifax was enthralled with the Western Wear stores. She wanted boots, belts, fringed shirts, all the tourist lures. I wouldn't play.

We turned onto a straggling side street and passed my old grade school, scene of so many golden childhood memories. If I pointed it out to Halifax, she'd just want to look closer, walk around, ask me questions I didn't want to answer. I said nothing.

We turned down another street and there was my ex-home. I glanced at it casually and said nothing. It had a new porch, new curtains, new paint,

contemporary-issues classes every semester. There are small but vocal groups of students who refuse to be invisible as queers, single mothers, people of colour, and/or disabled people.

But there has also been very palpable backlash against these groups in response to the gains they have made. There has been graphic death-threat graffiti against lesbians and gay men, in the toilets and halls of that liberal art school. There have been chilling personal attacks against the only First Nations teacher in the school, written on the walls of that teacher's classroom. The new usage of the term "politically correct" is one of the more polite manifestations of the backlash from the Right, which sees the changes of the last few decades as an overwhelming threat.

LIZARD: When I read about neo-Nazis complaining about their "curtailed freedom of expression," or "censored" academics who can no longer even promote sexual harassment (poor things), or men who refuse to be "silenced" by women talking about violence against women, I am struck dumb. I am so angry that I can barely respond enough to say I think this is crap. I feel powerless and furious.

There's no arguing about it, because there's no common basis for argument, there's not anything to agree on, the two ways of thinking are so different, it would be like arguing with someone from Mars who had learned the language but didn't understand the concepts. It reminds me of trying to argue with my parents when I was a child. They always had a comeback that seemed rational but *made no sense*. It didn't deal with anything that I was talking about.

These people I read about in the paper are not my parents. But they do have power, and I threaten it. And they are fighting back in the same indescribably frustrating way as my parents did, by saying they make sense, by being oh so reasonable and calm when really they are lashing out with the biggest weapons they can muster. And they are formidable weapons—the universities, the media, public funding, corporate power.

Is

this

sex?

new people. But the same old garage, spiders in the dark, the old smell of oil spilled one summer and cleaned up with sand, grit on my cheek, his hand on the back of my neck, pressing my face into the concrete floor.

My eyes filled with whirling black spots. Everything was getting smaller and farther away, and I was trying to breathe a brick wall. My knees wanted to give way, but Halifax was pulling me along the street, down the block, around the corner, away.

"Walk," she ordered. "Come on."

I was walking reasonably well on my own steam by the time we got back to the Bucking Bronco. Some ecologically sensitive person had turned off the air conditioner. My room was hot and dark. I lay down on the bed and she lay beside me, stroking my hair. That was nice. Maybe I'd go to sleep and wake up in Vancouver.

"So that was where you used to live, eh?" she said after a while. The bitch is too bright. I can't keep anything from her.

"I don't want to talk about it," I said.

But don't think I am fooled for one minute. I grew up with this. I grew up with the myth that there is such a thing as total objectivity, you just need the right judge. That there are universal principles that result in total equality. And anyone who doesn't agree with the particular ways they are interpreted is subversive.

For example, the principle is that professors should be allowed to express themselves. I agree. But when I apply this principle to real life, I don't agree with the interpretations I read. I have questions. Are those professors being *prevented* from expressing themselves? Are they willing to take responsibility for what they are saying? Can they deal with challenges to their authority? Do they believe everyone has the same right to self-expression as they do? If so, are they willing to hand over their lecture platforms? How much immunity from political debate comes with tenure?

But if you ask these questions, the comeback is that professors should be allowed to express themselves. I am tired of this predictability masquerading as an original response. It's the backlash, and we predicted it, and it's here. Think of something new to say.

I am tired of sloppy thinking masquerading as the "rational" side. I am tired of having statements by women's groups, anti-racist activists, disabled speakers, or lesbian artists be dismissed as hysterical, dogmatic, and narrow-minded (of all things). I can't think of a way to argue because it's the ultimate doublespeak, by people who think they control the power of the word.

Whose universe?

KISS & TELL: Equality is one of the "universal" principles of Euro-American liberalism. It was considered a universal principle way back when the only people allowed to vote on this continent were white male property owners. It was considered a universal principle when many people on this continent were living in slavery. Obviously, these universal principles are applied in particular ways, de-

"Okay."

She kissed my cheek and then my lips. I stared at the wall. My eyes were adjusting to the dark and I could just make out the pattern of the wallpaper. She snuggled closer to me, nuzzling my neck. Her hand brushed across my breasts, very soft, then down to my belly. Then back to my breasts. My nipples were hard. I lay frozen. She touched me again, again. Every touch went straight to my cunt. Her soft hands filled me with a terrible pain. I had never been so turned on in my life.

"Stop it," I whispered.

"Hmmm?"

"Stop it!" This time it was very loud. She stopped.

"What's wrong?" she asked.

"Fuck you," I said. It was all I could think of, so I said it again. Halifax leaned back on her elbow and looked at me.

"I get the impression you're not into sex right now," she said.

"Oh fuck off . . . just . . . don't . . . You act like

pending on who is involved, when and where. Some people are more equal than others.

These days, equality is still invoked in strange ways. For many people it means treating everyone exactly the same regardless of their circumstances and histories. As Anatole France said, "The law in its majestic equality forbids the rich as well as the poor to sleep under bridges, to beg in the streets, and to steal bread."

Under this definition of equality, affirmative action is called "reverse discrimination" because it doesn't pretend we're all the same. But ignoring our differences and our present-day lack of equality serves to entrench inequality.

"Universal" equality was recently invoked by a Canadian Legion branch that denied entrance to a group of Sikh veterans because they wouldn't take off their turbans. It wasn't racism, we were told; no one in their branch is allowed to wear "headgear" in the building. Everyone was being treated equally, and the Sikh veterans had the choice to either break their religious requirements or not take part in Remembrance Day ceremonies at the Legion. All people, regardless of race, are equally required to comply with that branch's interpretation of obscure Anglo customs, or stay out. And that's supposed to be equality.

The same kind of retreat to "universal" principles that calls affirmative action "reverse discrimination" is often used to dismiss the issue of cultural appropriation in art. Cultural appropriation refers to the practice of artists, writers, social scientists, and so on from a dominant culture building careers on images, stories, or information taken from cultures whose own art, writing, and social sciences are at the same time being suppressed. A clear example of this was given by Maria Campbell at the series of forums *Telling Our Own Story:*

> Much of the history of our people has been written by non-Native people. A few years ago in Alberta, a special department was set up in the University of Alberta and millions of dollars was poured into this

you're taking care of me and then you start . . . all that." The words didn't really make sense but they were spilling out. "You jerk. You creep. Just fuck off. Go away."

"I'm sorry," she said. "I thought you were into it."

"Stop acting nice. You don't care how I feel. Just go away!"

She got off the bed and sat on the luggage rack by the door. "I'm not trying to change the topic from how insensitive I was, but is there something else going on?"

"No," I said.

"Was it something to do with seeing your old house?"

"No," I said.

"Okay," she said. She sat there, quietly, watching me. I could hear a motorcycle in the distance. Or maybe a car with a bad muffler. The light in the room was pearly and soft with dark edges, sunshine through beige fibreglass curtains.

"It was the garage," I said.

"When you were a kid?"

project. The project involved non-Native people studying the writings and the history of our people. These were called "the Riel Papers." Not one penny of that was ever spent on encouraging Metis writers to do the work.[4]

People who argue against the practice of cultural appropriation are often called censors simply for asking dominant culture artists to act more responsibly. Campbell says:

> I know I keep hearing the word censorship. I hear it over and over when I talk about this and I think it's got nothing to do with censorship, it's got to do with ethics. I think it is stealing and there is no way you can get away from that.[5]

Arguments against cultural appropriation are rooted in specific situations in a specific time in history, past and present. They are not universal principles applied equally, across the board, in every situation for all time.

For example, in British Columbia, First Nations people were at one time arrested for participating in potlatch ceremonies. Many works of art were confiscated in those raids, art which later turned up in museums or the homes of white collectors. Later, institutions like the Vancouver Art Gallery refused to buy the work of First Nations artists who used traditional styles, saying it was anthropology, not art.[6] At the same time, the Gallery was buying work by white artists who used traditional First Nations forms and imagery in combination with European styles.

Often First Nations images or stories are used by white artists without any understanding of their context and meaning. Sometimes they are not only misunderstood, but misused, mistold, in ways that perpetuate oppressive stereotypes. In some First Nations cultures, there are images and stories that are the

4. Maria Campbell, quoted by Kerrie Charnley in the Final Report of a series of forums called "Telling Our Own Story: Appropriation and Indigenous Writers and Performing Artists," 1990, p. 13.

5. Maria Campbell, quoted in "Telling Our Own Story" Final Report, p. 20.

6. This policy, in place for decades, has now been changed, in response to the many arguments put forth by First Nations artists and theorists.

"Yeah."

"Who was it?"

"Some guy. A stranger."

"Do you want to tell me about it?"

"No," I said.

"Okay. Whatever you want to do. You're in charge."

I lay there, silent and stiff. She managed to look cool and relaxed on the rickety luggage rack, like she was ready to sit there for hours. She can always outwait me. It's not fair. I sat up.

"What I feel like doing is fucking," I said.

"Okay," she said. She crossed the room and sat on the side of the bed.

I moved away from her, as much as I could on the undersized motel mattress.

"But I also feel like yelling at you," I said.

"That's fine too."

"Yeah, well you're not my therapist! If I wanted a therapist I'd go get one, and I sure as hell wouldn't sleep with her, so don't pull that shit on me."

"Damn right I'm not your fucking therapist,"

exclusive property of particular families or clans. For anyone else to use them is an act similar to plagiarism or violating copyright law. All this (and more) is behind many First Nations people's demand for accountability from white artists in Canada. It has to do with a specific historical situation, where people's work has been stolen, where certain artists have been shut out while others profit, where harmful stereotypes are reinforced, where copyrights are broken and important cultural symbols are treated with ignorant disrespect.

People who call this position "censorship" often misrepresent (and misunderstand) it. They talk as if critics of cultural appropriation were setting up a Universal Principle of Cultural No Trespassing that states: "No one is allowed to make art based on the art forms of cultures not their own." Then they argue against that principle. They give examples of what would happen if it were applied equally to everyone. It would mean a Japanese musician shouldn't play Bach. It would mean a Hungarian dancer shouldn't perform an Irish jig.

These examples clearly show that any Universal Principle of Cultural No Trespassing is ridiculous. But they don't involve histories of invasion and present-day realities of suppression and exploitation. Cultural No Trespassing has *never* been what critics of cultural appropriation are arguing for. It's not an issue of Universal Principles. It's not about what has to happen everywhere, always and forever. It's about particular situations in particular places, and how we can move those situations on in a better direction.

I don't think anyone of us can claim to know the answers. I don't come here with answers for this question of appropriation or what we should be doing about it. All I know is that I see the damage that has happened with our people. And I can see that there is misrepresentation and there are lies that are being perpetuated and that's hurting not only our people but hurting all peoples. Because lies al-

she said. "Thank god!"

"I'd *never* have *you* for a therapist," I said.

She tried not to laugh and failed. I tried to be offended and failed.

"Jerk face," I said, pulling her down on the bed with me.

"Asshole," she said. "What do you want? You want to pretend sex is always easy? Sometimes stuff comes up in sex and some of it isn't just straight-up fun. If that makes you want to go away, fine, go away. But I'd rather talk, or cry, or fuck our way through it. That's not therapy, it's real life. I want *you*. Get it?"

I sighed and buried my face in her neck. She smelled of sweat and sex and sunscreen.

"It wasn't a stranger, it was my father," I said.

She started to say something, but I pushed her away from me. Then I pushed her off the bed. She lay on the floor, looking startled. I leaned over the edge of the bed and kissed her. Somehow in the middle of the kiss she ended up lying on top of me.

"You're in charge," she whispered.

ways destroy and cause chaos and replace truth, and we concern ourselves with that.

— JEANNETTE ARMSTRONG[7]

7. Jeannette Armstrong,
quoted in "Telling Our
Own Story" Final Report
(see note 4), pp. 19-20.

Whose freedom?

KISS & TELL: Black feminist theorist bell hooks' book of media and cultural
criticism, *Black Looks,* was seized by Canada Customs as possible hate literature
and therefore not allowed into Canada.

Meanwhile, efforts to get the Canadian military to deal with internal racism
are met with cries of censorship. When the right of people with social privilege
to say whatever they want, anytime, anywhere, is challenged, freedom of speech
is vigorously defended.

What this society considers to be fundamental truths, rights, and principles
have been defined and refined over decades, centuries. The people who have
been central in formulating these definitions have been white European men of
the middle and upper classes. Their biases are reflected in these concepts. Their
point of view is seen as universal rather than particular and limited.

One of the most blatant examples is how Man was for so long assumed to
include women, so that what was true of men became the Universal and what
was true of women was just a subcategory, a deviation from the norm.

PERSIMMON: I remember when I first started seeing the world from the point of
view of women. I had been female all 20 years of my life, but in subtle and far-
reaching ways, I still saw men as central and women as a subgroup. To abandon
that perspective was a wild and difficult shift.

Some ways of thinking are so ingrained that it's hard to even notice them,
particularly when we're on the comfortable side of the power imbalance. Challenges to this ideology are often unheard or ignored, because the biases of our

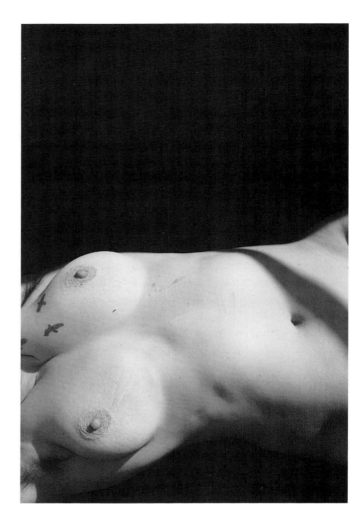

Whose

absence is guaranteed by

my presence?

"Touch me," I said.

She touched me, slow and soft like before.

"Hit me," I said.

Halifax paused for a fraction of a second and then slapped me hard across my face. The sudden pain shocked through my body and I cried out, clinging to her.

She looked into my face, searching. "You're so beautiful," she said and slapped me again.

"No, don't!" I flinched away from her.

She stayed where she was. "You're in charge."

I caught my breath. "Yes," I said. "Okay." I let the thought turn in my mind. "Get me a drink of water," I said.

She brought me a glass of water.

"Okay, kneel by the bed," I told her. She obeyed. Amazing. I was trying not to grin, but it was hard. I drank some water and then, on a second's impulse, I threw the rest in her face. She knelt there, water dripping down her neck. She looked very serious and sweet.

"Get on the bed," I said.

so-called universal truths are also the biases of most people who hold power, publish books, make laws.

In the white world, we act as if "race" is about people of colour, and white people's experience is apart from race. We don't notice our whiteness. We think it's all-pervasive and invisible, like air. But everyone else notices.

I notice how straight people forget that they're straight—for hours, days, years at a time. What luxury! Noticing that, I still forget I'm white. "As lesbians . . ." I say, and then I have to go back and think about it. Is it a lesbian thing or just a white lesbian thing? It's like trying to see when the eye doctor puts those weird drops in your eyes. It's like trying to wake up from a dream. But I'm working on it. The benefits of learning to see the world (and my own life) from a wider, more flexible, more realistic perspective are obvious.

As a lesbian, I'm quite familiar with straight perspectives on the world. I don't have to struggle to take them into account. I'm surrounded by images of hetero-sexuality. I learn to read myself into those pictures, change their meaning to include me. It's a subversive thing, but it doesn't challenge the right of hets to be seen as the universal norm, representing all people, while lesbians are different, particular, special (as in special rights, special-interest groups, special needs).

I grew up and live in a culture that encourages me to forget some things and won't allow me to forget others. In this book, my identity as a woman and a lesbian are always in the foreground, my identity as a Euro-Canadian comes in and out of focus, and having learning disabilities virtually disappears (even though the act of writing calls that identity up over and over). Parts of my identity jump out or are forgotten, depending on what I'm writing about. I can't always tell when that means I'm writing from a cultural blind spot, and when I'm just writing from a specific point of view.

But do I have to keep chopping up my identities, with some parts visible, others masquerading as universal, and still others dismissed as irrelevant? Do we

She obeyed. We lay together, kissing and feeling each other, till that terrible lovely pain rose in me again.

"Tie me up," I said.

She went to my suitcase and pulled out four long leather straps that I had certainly never packed.

She stretched me out on the bed, tying my wrists and ankles to the iron bedstead. She lay on top of me, touching my bound body softly, kissing my mouth. I wanted to hold her, touch her, but I was tied to the bed. A wild helplessness filled my chest, like panic, but sweeter.

When I was moaning under her, she got up and went back to my suitcase. She pulled out a knife.

"Don't!" I said. She stopped. I waited. She waited. I could see the pearly light on her cheek-bones, the line of her shoulders, her breasts under the tight T-shirt, her legs spread casually wide.

"No, it's okay," I said. "Do it."

She cut the buttons off my shirt, one by one, and opened it; cut my bra into pieces and threw it on the floor. She slit open my pants and pulled them

have to always speak as this fragment and that fragment? Does this language have the words to speak our simultaneous selves?

Covert censorship

PERSIMMON: In 1990, I spoke at the Canadian Museums Association Conference in Edmonton about right-wing attempts to cut funding to lesbian and gay artists. Many gay and lesbian arts administrators came up and introduced themselves to me over the weekend. But there were other people in town that weekend who weren't so warmly welcomed—a Native delegation from North Dakota was petitioning a local museum for the return of stolen artworks of deep religious significance. Their petition was turned down. The museum said it owned their heritage.

As I looked around that weekend, I saw that there were very few people of colour at that conference of influential arts administrators. There were far more white queers than there were people of colour—straight, gay, or whatever. The censorship of exclusion was alive and well, and at that level of the art world, white gays and lesbians were not the main target of it.

LIZARD: There are writers who have empowered me by articulating censorship issues in terms of problems I understand. Among them is U.S. writer and artist Carol Jacobsen,[8] who discusses covert censorship. It's the kind of censorship oppressed groups experience, where no one bans the work, exactly, it's just that it's not good enough to be published, or not appropriate for this gallery, or not the kind of job our print shop wants right now.

Toronto writer Marlene Nourbese Philip, in her 1989 essay "The Disappearing Debate,"[9] articulates the conflict between two anti-censorship battles: fighting for freedom of speech for individual writers, and fighting against systemic racism in publishing. Nourbese Philip sets her argument in the context of the debate then raging across Canada about the Women's Press' anti-racist guidelines.[10] Other examples are only too easy to find. In Canada in the 1990s, "free-

8. Carol Jacobsen, "Redefining Censorship: A Feminist View," *Art Journal* 50, no. 4 (1991): 42-55.

9. Marlene Nourbese Philip, "The Disappearing Debate, Or, how the Discussion of Racism Has Been Taken Over by the Censorship Issue," in her *Frontiers,* (Stratford, Ontario: The Mercury Press, 1992), 269-86.

10. In 1989 the Women's Press in Toronto rejected three stories from an anthology because they felt the stories were racist. They followed up the action by printing anti-racist guidelines for their writers.

dom of speech" is somehow seen as a *more* universal or fundamental principle than freedom from racism.

In her essay, Nourbese Philip dismantles the notion (especially appealing to white male artists) of an unfettered imagination driven inexorably by the muse, out of the artist's control, which must not be held to account by political concerns. She says:

> The imagination, I maintain, is both free and unfree. Free in that it can wander wheresoever it wishes, unfree in that it is profoundly affected and shaped by the societies in which we live.[11]

11. Marlene Nourbese Philip, "The Disappearing Debate," 278.

The censorship fence

LIZARD: I have been dragged kicking and screaming to an anti-censorship position. I did not start out here. I found the analysis logically compelling but politically lacking. I felt the anti-censorship position ignored a lot of things. For one thing, I was expected to believe that images are only symptoms, never causes, and never dangerous. It is a short step from that to building an alliance with Jim Keegstra,[12] and I refuse.

Over the censorship fence I have watched the pro-legislative reform feminists with some curiosity. Maybe it will work, I thought. Maybe they will really be able to stop sexism and leave sex intact. It seemed clear that any such legislation would be used against lesbians and gays, but a part of me wanted to believe otherwise, wanted to believe that it could work.

But it doesn't work. Right from the start, the most dire lesbian predictions have come true. The first implementation of Butler was the seizure of a lesbian magazine (*Bad Attitude*) at a gay bookstore (Glad Day Books in Toronto). Since then, Butler has been used against lesbians and gays over and over again.

So do we want to give up on law reform altogether, or do we want to keep pushing for the protection of laws, knowing the government has a different

12. Jim Keegstra was a high school history teacher who in the 1980s taught his students that the Holocaust never happened. He used freedom of speech arguments to defend his actions.

off. It was a sharp knife. I could tell. I lay there, tied open, exposed. She sat back, her eyes cruising my body. I waited. She waited.

My mouth was dry. My heart was pounding, pounding.

"Please," I said, and she slowly moved toward me. With the back of the knife blade, she stroked my nipples, first one, then the other, over and over. Fear and desire fought in my throat. My body was slick with sweat. My breath came fast and ragged.

She leaned over to the bedside table and pulled out a package of latex gloves. Maybe someone left them there, along with the Gideon's Bible. She pulled one on. It was shiny silver. Safer sex with style. She untied me, retied me ass up. I could feel her eyes on me. There was no way to hide. The back of her blade caressed my butt, and then suddenly the edge, swift and sharp. I gasped and twisted my tied body so I could see her over my shoulder. Her face was hard and beautiful. She parted the cheeks of my ass and her knife whispered across my crack. Slowly, she slipped a

agenda from ours? What about the people who are hurt by the laws? What about the people who are hurt by the lack of laws? Are we going to weigh their relative pain and decide? Who is going to decide?

13. Noam Chomsky, in the film *Manufacturing Consent,* by Mark Achbar and Peter Wintonick (co-produced by Necessary Illusions and the National Film Board, 1992).

KISS & TELL: The censorship debate has forged unthinkable alliances. There are the women who built a common front with the political Right to make the Butler decision. And there are the Noam Chomskys[13] of the world, who insist that we anti-censorship activists have to protect books by neo-fascists like LePen in order to be consistent. In both cases we have been told that distasteful as these alliances are, they are necessary.

But maybe these alliances are only necessary if the world is divided in two by the present censorship fence. The discussion of censorship, criticism, affirmative action, regulation, reform, and imagery is much more complicated than this debate allows. There are other ways to look at it, that make more sense, that make the pieces fit better.

When we talk about censorship we need to talk about power—who has it, and what are they doing with it? We have to look at each instance and weigh the power imbalances. Who has the power to speak? Who has the power to impose silence? Who has the law on their side? Who has economic power on their side? Who has media control on their side? Who has gallery control on their side? Who will go to jail? Who is trying to redress what?

In Canada today, we are not equal. Many people are not free to speak, free from discrimination, free from poverty. Freedom and equality aren't abstract concepts separate from daily life. They can't be laid over the power imbalances of our present system without being distorted beyond all meaning. The fight against censorship only makes sense when these realities are not denied.

finger up my ass, and then out. My cunt was open, wet, yearning toward her, but she ignored it. Her fingers were slick with lube from somewhere, nowhere. Two fingers now up my tight hot hole, burning inside me, filling me with fire. I couldn't breathe. She pushed into me, slowly, slowly, taking me moaning, crying, tied writhing on the harsh sheets. The impossibly slow strokes, her knife, her mouth. She had me, held me, hurt me. I was hers.

AFTERWORD

SUSAN: What is this preoccupation with and passion for making images and representations? We've talked about why we continue to do the things we do. Why we take our clothes off for cameras, why we rummage through our pasts and expose ourselves, why we keep poking and prodding at the censorship debates, why the sex, sex, sex. Yet what part does art play in all of this?

Sometimes it feels like the art part gets lost in the shuffle. We get so busy explaining ourselves, managing productions, keeping up with the reactions to our work, organizing gigs, dealing with censorship issues, that sometimes we lose sight of some of the basic motivations that brought us to do the work in the first place. We forget what it feels like to engage with the process of art, the wild intoxication of finally, finally finding/making/creating a space where we can make room for our enormous need to explore. A place where the only rules are the ones we set ourselves. A place where we give ourselves permission to say the truth no matter how fucked-up that truth can feel, how out of sync with what we've been told.

Art-making in its myriad forms is also a place where we can push the possibilities of media and sometimes break through our everyday vision. For me, looking through a camera is an exercise in framing off what is seen in new and unexpected ways. Despite the tyranny of the frame and the system it stands for, there is the window of possibility that the lens offers: through that tiny viewfinder anything can happen. Or standing in front of an audience knowing that these shared moments are utterly unique, will never recur exactly the same way and that all of us, performers and audience alike, may be changed through our interaction. It is this revolutionary *potential* that keeps us motivated.

Why all the sex? Simply because we are queer and to be queer means to be defined by sexual difference. Since this *difference* is the raison d'être of the social discrimination and invisibility we endure in this culture, it should come as no surprise that some of us choose to deal with sexuality in our work. The act of representing something that is given zero value (lesbianism) and representing it in such a way that it has unmistakable meaning as *difference* throws into question the omnipotence of a system that denies the very possiblilty of that difference. *Women* are defined through their relationship to *men*. Representations of lesbians open up possibilities for women, possibilities which are outside of that definition.

The trick, of course, is how to make a representation that has this effect, given that whenever we see images of women in popular culture they are assumed to be heterosexual. These images don't need any explanation because we've seen them a zillion times before. We've been living under patriarchal rule so long it's hard to imagine ways in which predetermined, concretized notions of how women look can be significantly altered, no matter who they are next to or what they are doing *with* who they are next to. Women are still in a subordinate relation to dominant culture (Big Daddy) no matter who their personal relationships are with.

One of Kiss & Tell's strategies has been to begin making images, despite the contradictions. Images that start to articulate a kind of lesbian imaginary, even when it seems an act of pure invention. The difficulty is in articulating this into something that makes patriarchal references clear, and creating meaning that can be read as lesbian even by the non-lesbian viewer. To complicate the task, the means of production carry their own weight of ideological baggage that must be both identified and subverted. That is why we like to show our crew, our untidy closets, our complicated histories, and it is why we put so much emphasis on collaboration and process. None of this is simple. It is inconclusive and unresolved, and we end up with more questions than answers. It is, however, a place to work.

Kiss & Tell is a collective of three lesbian artists in Vancouver, Canada who have been working together for more than nine years on issues of sexuality and representation. They have created and performed several explicit sexual works, including DRAWING THE LINE, an interactive photo exhibit, and TRUE INVERSIONS, a multi-media performance.

The postcard book DRAWING THE LINE, also published by Press Gang Publishers, includes 40 images from the photo exhibit and comments from women in five cities. For information on the book, exhibit or performance, contact Kiss & Tell through Press Gang Publishers.

The DRAWING THE LINE video, produced and directed by Lorna Boschman, is a 7-minute documentary of the photo exhibit. The TRUE INVERSIONS video, written and produced by Kiss & Tell, directed by Lorna Boschman, is a 30-minute video about imagery, censorship, and lesbian sex. It is also used as part of the multi-media performance. To rent or purchase either video, contact Video Out, 1965 Main St., Vancouver, B.C., Canada V5T 3C1. Telephone: (604) 872-8449; Fax: (604) 876-1185.

Persimmon Blackbridge is a well-known learning-disabled-lesbian-cleaning-lady-white-sculptor-writer-performance-and-media artist. Over the last 20 years, her work has been rooted in lesbian and psychiatric survivors' movement activism. Much of her art (including *Still Sane, Doing Time,* and *Sunnybrook*) has explored Canadian institutions such as prisons and mental hospitals, both from her own experience as an outpatient, and in collaboration with ex-inmates.

Lizard Jones is an interdisciplinary artist and performer, with a background in grassroots social activism and the alternative media. Aside from Kiss & Tell, she is also active in the Association for Noncommercial Culture, which is a group of artists producing public art with a political focus. She has worked as a graphic designer, a freelance writer, an editor, and many things in between.

Interdisciplinary artist **Susan Stewart** has been producing photography and multimedia performance works since 1978. She also teaches and has an M.F.A. from Simon Fraser University. Her most recent work, *Lovers & Warriors: aural/photographic collaborations,* was an installation produced in collaboration with 25 women, mostly lesbians, which explores issues of gender, marginality, and the politics of photographic representation.

PRESS GANG PUBLISHERS FEMINIST CO-OPERATIVE is committed to producing quality books with social and literary merit. We give priority to Canadian women's work and include writing by lesbians and by women of diverse cultural and class backgrounds. Our list features vital and provocative fiction, poetry and non-fiction. A free catalogue is available from Press Gang Publishers, #101 - 225 East 17th Ave., Vancouver, B.C., Canada V5V 1A6.